DATE DUE		

ISLAMIC
FUNDAMENTALISM

Other books in the At Issue series:

ISLAMIC FUNDAMENTALISM

Auriana Ojeda, *Book Editor*

Daniel Leone, *President*
Bonnie Szumski, *Publisher*
Scott Barbour, *Managing Editor*

San Diego • Detroit • New York • San Francisco • Cleveland
New Haven, Conn. • Waterville, Maine • London • Munich

THOMSON
━━━★━━━ ™
GALE

For more information, contact
Greenhaven Press
27500 Drake Rd.
Farmington Hills, MI 48331-3535
Or you can visit our Internet site at http://www.gale.com

LIBRARY OF CONGRESS CATALOGING-IN-PUBLICATION DATA

Islamic fundamentalism / Auriana Ojeda, book editor.
    p. cm. — (At issue)
  Includes bibliographical references and index.
  ISBN 0-7377-1330-5 (lib. bdg. : alk. paper) —
  ISBN 0-7377-1331-3 (pbk. : alk. paper)
    1. Islamic fundamentalism. 2. Terrorism—Religious aspects—Islam. 3. Islam and politics. 4. Islam—20th century. I. Ojeda, Auriana, 1977– . II. At issue (San Diego, Calif.)
  BP163 .I776 2003
  297'.09'051—dc21   2002070612

Contents

Introduction

In 1993, Islamic terrorists bombed the World Trade Center in New York City, killing 7 people and injuring more than 1,000. In 1995, 19 Americans were killed and 500 were injured when Islamic terrorists blew up American barracks in Saudi Arabia. Islamic terrorists bombed U.S. embassies in Kenya and Tanzania simultaneously in 1998, killing 258 and wounding more than 5,000. Seventeen U.S. servicemen were killed when Islamic terrorists bombed the USS *Cole* at a Yemen port in 2000. In 2001, Islamic terrorists hijacked four U.S. airliners and crashed them into the World Trade Center towers, the Pentagon, and rural Pennsylvania, killing more than 3,000 people.

These and other terrorist attacks contribute, not unreasonably, to the Western perception that all Muslims are anti-American terrorists. Terrorist attacks receive enormous media attention, and most Americans base their views of Muslims on the stories they hear on the news. To be sure, most Westerners are unaware of Muslim customs and ideologies, except for what they learn from the media. It is important to acknowledge that not all Muslims are fundamentalists, and not all fundamentalists are terrorists. However, fundamentalism, by its very nature, carries the threat of extremism, and extremism can easily morph into violence. Islamic fundamentalists can therefore pose a terrorist threat to their enemies. Unfortunately, many Middle Easterners perceive America as an enemy. Knowing the principles of Islam is the first step toward understanding how Islamic fundamentalism can lead to terrorism.

Islam is the fastest growing religion in the world and is second only to Christianity in number of adherents. Muslims live in all parts of the world, but the majority of Muslims are concentrated in the Middle East and Asia. Islam has two meanings: Peace, and submission to Allah (God). Muslims believe that Islam is the only true religion and that it was revealed by the prophet Muhammad in Arabia in the seventh century. Pious Muslims adhere to the five pillars of Islam: acknowledging that there is no true god except God and that Muhammad is the prophet of God; praying five times a day toward Mecca; giving alms to the poor; fasting during the month of Ramadan (the ninth month of the lunar year); and for those who are financially and physically able, making an annual pilgrimage to Mecca. Islam also requires belief in six articles of faith, which are belief in God, belief in the messengers and prophets of God, belief in the Revelations and the Koran (the Islamic holy book), belief in angels, belief in Judgment Day, and belief in the ultimate power of God or God's decree. Other precepts of Islam are concerned with matters such as diet, clothing, personal hygiene, business ethics, responsibilities toward parents, spouses, and children, marriage, divorce, inheritance, civil and criminal law, fighting in defense of Islam, relations with non-Muslims, and much more.

All Muslims believe in the six articles of faith and adhere to the five pillars of Islam, but they differ in how they interpret the Koran and the *shari'a* (Islamic law). Colonel B.S. Burmeister, in his essay "The Rise of Islamic Fundamentalism," identified two major divisions within Islam, the modernists and the revivalists. He argues that modernists believe in the inerrancy of the Koran, but they interpret its strictures in a modern context. Modernists accept secular governments, religious diversity, and the emancipation of women. Most Muslim modernists condemn terrorism and advocate individual relationships with God. On the other hand, revivalists favor a literal interpretation of the Koran and a return to traditional Islamic ideas. These Muslims are extremely pious and closely follow the teachings of the Koran and Muhammad. They regularly attend mosques, and many promote a theocratic government and enforcement of the *shari'a*. Revivalists are frequently referred to as Islamists or Islamic fundamentalists.

The term *fundamentalism* as it applies to religion generally was derived from a series of essays published in the United States from 1910 to 1915 by Christian evangelists. The authors intended to promote the literal interpretation of the Bible and reject concessions that were being made to modern scientific theory and philosophy. According to Macksood Aftab, managing editor of the *Islamic Herald*, "The term Fundamentalist, in the Christian world, is synonymous with the 'Bible thumpers' and the televangelists." Recently, the term has been used by Westerners to describe Muslims who promote strict adherence to traditional Islamic tenets. Bahman Baktiari, a political science professor at the American University in Cairo, contends that there is no word for fundamentalism in Arabic. Baktiari states that Islamic fundamentalism is a purely Western construct, "used to describe the rise of Islamic forces in the Middle East."

Religious fundamentalists believe in the absolute inerrancy of their sacred texts and religious leaders. Their beliefs do not automatically translate into terrorism, but the passion and conviction that are inherent in fundamentalism teeter on the edge of extremism. Extremism or radicalism in any belief system often leads to violence because its adherents dogmatically adhere to their beliefs and consider conflicting beliefs threatening. For example, America has witnessed several acts of terrorism in the name of Christian fundamentalism, such as the bombings of abortion clinics and shootings of abortion providers. Islamic extremists manifest the same conviction and self-assurance as Christian extremists.

Much Islamic extremism stems from a sense of displacement and alienation from the modern world. Among the many reasons for this perception is the steady decline of Islamic civilization since the Middle Ages. During Europe's Dark Ages, Islam flourished, recording many cultural, political, literary, educational, and artistic achievements. However, Islam has declined in strength and influence since the end of the Crusades around 1500. Today, many Muslim countries suffer in extremely impoverished, unstable, and war-torn conditions. For example, Afghanistan today has the highest infant, child, and maternal mortality rates, and the lowest literacy and life expectancy rates in the world. Afghanistan's per capita income is estimated at about $200 for a nation of 23 million. By contrast, the per capita income in America is approximately $24,000. Many Islamic extremists blame these conditions on Western imperialism and culture.

Western presence in the Middle East planted the seeds for Islamic fundamentalism in that region during Europe's colonial period. Beginning around the end of the eighteenth century, major European powers invaded and colonized nearly all North African and Middle Eastern countries. Europe pursued military and economic dominance over the region until the close of World War II, when a series of coups and revolutions brought nationalist governments to power in the region. Muslims resented Europe's oppressive colonial power and the contempt that Westerners had for Middle Eastern civilization.

In the second half of the twentieth century, Arab Muslims unsuccessfully attempted to create solidarity among the Arab nations (Pan-Arabism). When this strategy failed, many people turned to a burgeoning movement in fundamentalism. The movement gained power after the establishment of the state of Israel on Palestinian land in 1948, which many Muslims refer to as the "catastrophe." The Cold War period from 1949 to 1989 fueled anti-Western sentiment, as Muslims saw Westerners, especially Americans, fund regimes that protected their own interests. The United States, for example, supported regimes that protected its oil supply and opposed communism. In addition, many Muslims resent the continued presence of Americans on Saudi Arabian lands after the Gulf War ended. According to terrorist Osama bin Laden, "The call to wage war against America was made because America has spear-headed the crusade against the Islamic nation, sending tens of thousands of its troops to the land of the two Holy Mosques over and above its meddling in its affairs and its politics, and its support of the oppressive, corrupt and tyrannical regime that is in control."

Along with the physical presence of the United States in the Middle East, many Muslims resent American culture. Many Islamic fundamentalists argue that their culture has been subsumed by American culture, which, as a result of technology, spread rapidly throughout the world during the second half of the twentieth century. Islamic fundamentalists see Westerners as unholy and decadent, especially the Western media. They despise American immodesty and secularism, and some Islamic fundamentalist regimes, like the Taliban in Afghanistan (which was toppled by American troops during the U.S. war against terrorism), banned televisions, radios, and music to restrict non-Muslim influence in their nations. Radical Muslims contend that the spread of Western culture into the Middle East contributes to its poverty and social problems.

According to radical Muslims, things have gone wrong in Islamic countries because they have strayed from the basic principles and traditional practices of Islam. Moreover, Western presence and influence contributed to Muslims' deviance from the righteous path. Therefore, Islamic extremists argue that Muslims must expel Westerners from Muslim homelands, reject Western politics and customs, and return to a literal interpretation of the Koran and Muhammad's teachings.

Furthermore, since Islamic fundamentalists maintain that Islam is the one true religion, extremists advocate overthrowing powerful secular governments and replacing them with a single Islamic authority. According to Bassam Tibi, one of the world's foremost specialists on Islamic fundamentalism, "The goal of Islamic fundamentalists is to abolish the Western, secular world order and replace it with a new Islamist divine order. . . . The goal of Islamists is a new imperial, absolutist Islamic world power." Islamic fundamentalists maintain that one of their duties as Muslims is to defend Islam from its enemies. Islamic extremists contend that Western powers—especially the United States, whom many fundamentalists characterize as the "Great Satan"—are enemies of Islam. According to Burmeister, mullahs have declared that any action taken on behalf of Islam is acceptable to God. By this rationale, Islamic extremists justify their acts of terrorism toward Westerners. Most extremists regard terrorist action toward the West as retribution for the atrocities that Western military committed in the Middle East. According to bin Laden, "The terrorism we practice is of the commendable kind for it is directed at the tyrants and the aggressors and the enemies of Allah. . . . Terrorizing those and punishing them are necessary measures to straighten things and to make them right. Tyrants and oppressors who subject the Arab nation to aggression ought to be punished. . . . America heads the list of aggressors against Muslims."

The specter of radical Islamists dominating the secular world is frightening, especially in light of recent terrorist attacks, but it is important to remember that most Muslims are not radical and that most espouse a modernist interpretation of the Koran and Islamic traditions. Islamic extremists represent a small faction of Muslims who, although influential, are probably not powerful enough to overthrow world superpowers. The majority of Muslims, especially those who live in the United States, are moderate, and they accept and value secular societies. These Muslims represent a compromise between Western and Islamic customs that celebrates cultural identity and tolerance. *At Issue: Islamic Fundamentalism* gives readers a thorough understanding of the issues surrounding fundamentalist Islam and how it relates to the West.

1

The Difference Between Islam and Islamic Fundamentalism

Daniel Pipes

Daniel Pipes is the director of the Middle East Forum, a think tank that works to define and promote American interests in the Middle East, and a columnist for both the New York Times *and the* Jerusalem Post. *He has written numerous books, including* Militant Islam Reaches America, In the Path of God: Islam and Political Power, *and* Slave Soldiers and Islam.

Islam is a complex faith that celebrates a rich culture and history in the Middle East and should not be confused with Islamic fundamentalism, a modern permutation of Islam. Muslims—as adherents of Islam are called—have devised three political responses to modernity. Secularists emulate the West, reformists appropriate some aspects of Western culture without acknowledging it, and fundamentalists reject Western influences. Islamic fundamentalism, or Islamism, champions returning to the fundamentals of Islam and the *shari'a* (Islamic law), rejecting Western culture and government, and transforming their faith into a political ideology. Indeed, Islamists use the state to promote their doctrines. Islamism differs from traditional Islam in that fundamentalists eagerly challenge the modern world, while traditionalists shy away from it. Islamism has been increasing for the last quarter century, and its adherents seek worldwide power and domination.

One cannot emphasize too much the distinction between Islam—plain Islam—and its fundamentalist version. Islam is the religion of about one billion people and is a rapidly growing faith, particularly in Africa but also elsewhere in the world. The United States, for example, boasts almost a million converts to Islam (plus an even larger number of Muslim immigrants).

Islam's adherents find their faith immensely appealing, for the religion possesses an inner strength that is quite extraordinary. As a leading figure in the Islamic Republic of Iran maintains, "Any Westerner who really understands Islam will envy the lives of Muslims." Far from feeling embarrassed about its being temporally the last of the three major Middle Eastern monotheisms, Muslims believe that their faith improves on the earlier ones. In their telling, Judaism and Christianity are but defective variants of Islam, which is God's final, perfect religion.

Contributing to this internal confidence is the memory of outstanding achievements during Islam's first six or so centuries. Its culture was the most advanced, and Muslims enjoyed the best health, lived the longest, had the highest rates of literacy, sponsored the most advanced scientific and technical research, and deployed usually victorious armies. This pattern of success was evident from the beginning: in A.D. 622 the Prophet Muhammad fled Mecca as a refugee, only to return eight years later as its ruler. As early as the year 715, Muslim conquerors had assembled an empire that extended from Spain in the west to India in the east. To be a Muslim meant to belong to a winning civilization. Muslims, not surprisingly, came to assume a correlation between their faith and their worldly success, to assume that they were the favored of God in both spiritual and mundane matters.

Muslims have devised three political responses to modernity—secularism, reformism, and Islamism.

And yet, in modern times battlefield victories and prosperity have been notably lacking. Indeed, as early as the thirteenth century, Islam's atrophy and Christendom's advances were already becoming discernible. But, for some five hundred years longer, Muslims remained largely oblivious to the extraordinary developments taking place to their north. Ibn Khaldun, the famous Muslim intellectual, wrote around the year 1400 about Europe, "I hear that many developments are taking place in the land of the Rum, but God only knows what happens there!"

Such willful ignorance rendered Muslims vulnerable when they could no longer ignore what was happening around them. Perhaps the most dramatic alert came in July 1798, when Napoleon Bonaparte landed in Egypt—the center of the Muslim world—and conquered it with stunning ease. Other assaults followed over the next century and more, and before long most Muslims were living under European rule. As their power and influence waned, a sense of incomprehension spread among Muslims. What had gone wrong? Why had God seemingly abandoned them?

The trauma of modern Islam results from this sharp and unmistakable contrast between medieval successes and more recent tribulations. Put simply, Muslims have had an exceedingly hard time explaining what went wrong. Nor has the passage of time made this task any easier, for the same unhappy circumstances basically still exist. Whatever index one employs, Muslims can be found clustering toward the bottom—whether measured in terms of their military prowess, political stability, economic development, corruption, human rights, health, longevity or literacy. Anwar Ibrahim, the former deputy prime minister of Malaysia who now languishes in jail, estimates in *The Asian Renaissance* (1997) that whereas Muslims make up just one-fifth of the world's total population, they constitute more than half of the 1.2 billion people living in abject poverty. There is thus a pervasive sense of debilitation and encroachment in the Islamic world today. As the imam of a mosque in Jerusalem put it not long ago, "Before, we were masters of the world and now we're not even masters of our own mosques."

Searching for explanations for their predicament, Muslims have devised three political responses to modernity—secularism, reformism and Islamism. The first of these holds that Muslims can only advance by emulating the West. Yes, the secularists concede, Islam is a valuable and esteemed legacy, but its public dimensions must be put aside. In particular, the sacred law of Islam (called the Shari'a)—which governs such matters as the judicial system, the manner in which Muslim states go to war, and the nature of social interactions between men and women—should be discarded in its entirety. The leading secular country is Turkey, where Kemal Ataturk in the period 1923–38 reshaped and modernized an overwhelmingly Muslim society. Overall, though, secularism is a minority position among Muslims, and even in Turkey it is under siege.

Reformism, occupying a murky middle ground, offers a more popular response to modernity. Whereas secularism forthrightly calls for learning from the West, reformism selectively appropriates from it. The reformist says, "Look, Islam is basically compatible with Western ways. It's just that we lost track of our own achievements, which the West exploited. We must now go back to our own ways by adopting those of the West." To reach this conclusion, reformers reread the Islamic scriptures in a Western light. For example, the Koran permits a man to take up to four wives—on the condition that he treat them equitably. Traditionally, and quite logically, Muslims understood this verse as permission for a man to take four wives. But because a man is allowed only one in the West, the reformists performed a sleight of hand and interpreted the verse in a new way: the Koran, they claim, requires that a man must treat his wives equitably, which is clearly something no man can do if there is more than one of them. So, they conclude, Islam prohibits more than a single wife.

Reformists have applied this sort of reasoning across the board. To science, for example, they contend Muslims should have no objections, for science is in fact Muslim. They recall that the word algebra comes from the Arabic, al-jabr. Algebra being the essence of mathematics and mathematics being the essence of science, all of modern science and technology thereby stems from work done by Muslims. So there is no reason to resist Western science; it is rather a matter of reclaiming what the West took (or stole) in the first place. In case after case, and with varying degrees of credibility, reformists appropriate Western ways under the guise of drawing on their own heritage. The aim of the reformists, then, is to imitate the West without acknowledging as much. Though intellectually bankrupt, reformism functions well as a political strategy.

The ideological response

The third response to the modern trauma is Islamism, the subject of the remainder of this essay. Islamism has three main features: a devotion to the sacred law, a rejection of Western influences, and the transformation of faith into ideology.

Islamism holds that Muslims lag behind the West because they're not good Muslims. To regain lost glory requires a return to old ways, and that is achieved by living fully in accordance with the Shari'a. Were Muslims to do so, they would once again reside on top of the world, as they did a millennium ago. This, however, is no easy task, for the sacred law contains a vast body of regulations touching every aspect of life, many of them contrary to modern practices. (The Shari'a somewhat resembles Jewish law, but nothing comparable exists in Christianity.) Thus, it forbids usury or any taking of interest, which has deep and obvious implications for economic life. It calls for cutting off the hands of thieves, which runs contrary to all modern sensibilities, as do its mandatory covering of women and the separation of the sexes. Islamism not only calls for the application of these laws, but for a more rigorous application than ever before was the case. Before 1800, the interpreters of the Shari'a softened it somewhat. For instance, they devised a method by which to avoid the ban on interest. The fundamentalists reject such modifications, demanding instead that Muslims apply the Shari'a strictly and in its totality.

Islamism represents an Islamic-flavored version of the radical utopian ideas of our time.

In their effort to build a way of life based purely on the Shari'a laws, Islamists strain to reject all aspects of Western influence—customs, philosophy, political institutions and values. Despite these efforts, they still absorb vast amounts from the West in endless ways. For one, they need modern technology, especially its military and medical applications. For another, they themselves tend to be modern individuals, and so are far more imbued with Western ways than they wish to be or will ever acknowledge. Thus, while the Ayatollah Khomeini, who was more traditional than most Islamists, attempted to found a government on the pure principles of Shiite Islam, he ended up with a republic based on a constitution that represents a nation via the decisions of a parliament, which is in turn chosen through popular elections—every one of these a Western concept. Another example of Western influence is that Friday, which in Islam is not a day of rest but a day of congregation, is now the Muslim equivalent of a sabbath. Similarly, the laws of Islam do not apply to everyone living within a geographical territory but only to Muslims; Islamists, however, understand them as territorial in nature (as an Italian priest living in Sudan found out long ago, when he was flogged for possessing alcohol). Islamism thereby stealthily appropriates from the West while denying that it is doing so.

Perhaps the most important of these borrowings is the emulation of Western ideologies. The word "Islamism" is a useful and accurate one, for it indicates that this phenomenon is an "ism" comparable to other ideologies of the twentieth century. In fact, Islamism represents an Islamic-flavored version of the radical utopian ideas of our time, following Marxism-Leninism and fascism. It infuses a vast array of Western political and economic ideas within the religion of Islam. As an Islamist, a Muslim Brother from Egypt, puts it, "We are neither socialist nor capitalist, but Muslims"; a Muslim of old would have said, "We are neither Jews nor Christians, but Muslims."

Islamists see their adherence to Islam primarily as a form of political allegiance; hence, though usually pious Muslims, they need not be. Plenty of Islamists seem in fact to be rather impious. For instance, the mastermind of the 1993 World Trade Center bombing in New York, Ramzi Yousef, had a girlfriend while living in the Philippines and was "gallivanting around Manila's bars, strip joints and karaoke clubs, flirting with women." From this and other suggestions of loose living, his biographer, Simon Reeve, finds "scant evidence to support any description of Yousef as a religious warrior." The FBI agent in charge of investigating Yousef concluded that, "He hid behind a cloak of Islam."

On a grander level, Ayatollah Khomeini hinted at the irrelevance of faith for Islamists in a letter to Mikhail Gorbachev early in 1989, as the Soviet Union was rapidly failing. The Iranian leader offered his own government as a model: "I openly announce that the Islamic Republic of Iran, as the greatest and most powerful base of the Islamic world, can easily help fill up the ideological vacuum of your system." Khomeini here seemed to be suggesting that the Soviets should turn to the Islamist ideology—converting to Islam would almost seem to be an afterthought.

Contrary to its reputation, Islamism is not a way back; as a contemporary ideology it offers not a means to return to some old-fashioned way of life but a way of navigating the shoals of modernization. With few exceptions (notably, the Taliban in Afghanistan), Islamists are city dwellers trying to cope with the problems of modern urban life—not people of the countryside. Thus, the challenges facing career women figure prominently in Islamist discussions. What, for example, can a woman who must travel by crowded public transportation do to protect herself from groping? The Islamists have a ready reply: she should cover herself, body and face, and signal through the wearing of Islamic clothes that she is not approachable. More broadly, they offer an inclusive and alternative way of life for modern persons, one that rejects the whole complex of popular culture, consumerism and individualism in favor of a faith-based totalitarianism.

Deviations from tradition

While Islamism is often seen as a form of traditional Islam, it is something profoundly different. Traditional Islam seeks to teach humans how to live in accord with God's will, whereas Islamism aspires to create a new order. The first is self-confident, the second deeply defensive. The one emphasizes individuals, the latter communities. The former is a personal credo, the latter a political ideology.

The distinction becomes sharpest when one compares the two sets of leaders. Traditionalists go through a static and lengthy course of learning in which they study a huge corpus of information and imbibe the Islamic verities much as their ancestors did centuries earlier. Their faith reflects more than a millennium of debate among scholars, jurists and theologians. Islamist leaders, by contrast, tend to be well educated in the sciences but not in Islam; in their early adulthood, they confront problems for which their modern learning has failed to prepare them, so they turn to Islam. In doing so they ignore nearly the entire corpus of Islamic learning and interpret the Koran as they see fit. As autodidacts, they dismiss the traditions and apply their own (modern) sensibilities to the ancient texts, leading to an oddly Protestant version of Islam.

[Traditional Muslims] fear the West while Islamists are eager to challenge it.

The modern world frustrates and stymies traditional figures who, educated in old-fashioned subjects, have not studied European languages, spent time in the West, or mastered its secrets. For example, traditionalists rarely know how to exploit the radio, television and the Internet to spread their message. In contrast, Islamist leaders usually speak Western languages, often have lived abroad, and tend to be well versed in technology. The Internet has hundreds of Islamist sites. Francois Burgat and William Dowell note this contrast in their book, *The Islamist Movement in North Africa* (1993):

> The village elder, who is close to the religious establishment and knows little of Western culture (from which he refuses technology a priori) cannot be confused with the young science student who is more than able to deliver a criticism of Western values, with which he is familiar and from which he is able to appropriate certain dimensions. The traditionalist will reject television, afraid of the devastating modernism that it will bring; the Islamist calls for increasing the number of sets . . . once he has gained control of the broadcasts.

Most important from our perspective, traditionalists fear the West while Islamists are eager to challenge it. The late mufti of Saudi Arabia, Abd al-'Aziz Bin-Baz, exemplified the tremulous old guard. In the summer of 1995, he warned Saudi youth not to travel to the West for vacation because "there is a deadly poison in travelling to the land of the infidels and there are schemes by the enemies of Islam to lure Muslims away from their religion, to create doubts about their beliefs, and to spread sedition among them." He urged the young to spend their summers in the "safety" of the summer resorts in their own country.

Islamists are not completely impervious to the fear of these schemes and lures, but they have ambitions to tame the West, something they do not shy from announcing for the whole world to hear. The most crude simply want to kill Westerners. In a remarkable statement, a Tunisian convicted of setting off bombs in France in 1985–86, killing thirteen, told the judge handling his case, "I do not renounce my fight against the West which assassinated the Prophet Muhammad. We Muslims should kill every last one of you [Westerners]." Others plan to expand Islam to Europe and America, using violence if necessary. An Amsterdam-based imam declared on a Turkish television program, "You must kill those who oppose Islam, the order of Islam or Allah, and His Prophet; hang or slaughter them

after tying their hands and feet crosswise . . . as prescribed by the Shari'a."
An Algerian terrorist group, the GIA, issued a communique in 1995 that
showed the Eiffel Tower exploding and bristled with threats:

> We are continuing with all our strength our steps of jihad
> and military attacks, and this time in the heart of France
> and its largest cities. . . . It's a pledge that [the French] will
> have no more sleep and no more leisure and Islam will en-
> ter France whether they like it or not.

The more moderate Islamists plan to use non-violent means to transform their host countries into Islamic states. For them, conversion is the
key. One leading American Muslim thinker, Ismail R. Al-Faruqi, put this
sentiment rather poetically: "Nothing could be greater than this youthful, vigorous and rich continent [of North America] turning away from its
past evil and marching forward under the banner of Allahu Akbar [God is
great]."

This contrast not only implies that Islamism threatens the West in a
way that the traditional faith does not, but it also suggests why traditional Muslims, who are often the first victims of Islamism, express contempt for the ideology. Thus, Naguib Mahfouz, Egypt's Nobel Prize winner for literature, commented after being stabbed in the neck by an
Islamist: "I pray to God to make the police victorious over terrorism and
to purify Egypt from this evil, in defense of people, freedom, and Islam."
Tujan Faysal, a female member of the Jordanian parliament, calls Islamism "one of the greatest dangers facing our society" and compares it
to "a cancer" that "has to be surgically removed." Cevik Bir, one of the
key figures in dispatching Turkey's Islamist government in 1997, flatly
states that in his country, "Muslim fundamentalism remains public enemy number one." If Muslims feel this way, so can non-Muslims; being
anti-Islamism in no way implies being anti-Islam.

Islamism in practice

Like other radical ideologues, Islamists look to the state as the main ve-
hicle for promoting their program. Indeed, given the impractical nature
of their scheme, the levers of the state are critical to the realization of
their aims. Toward this end, Islamists often lead political opposition parties (Egypt, Turkey, Saudi Arabia) or have gained significant power
(Lebanon, Pakistan, Malaysia). Their tactics are often murderous. In Algeria, an Islamist insurgency led to some 70,000 deaths from 1992 to 2000.

And when Islamists do take power, as in Iran, Sudan and Afghanistan,
the result is invariably a disaster. Economic decline begins immediately.
Iran, where for two decades the standard of living has almost relentlessly
declined, offers the most striking example of this. Personal rights are dis-
regarded, as spectacularly shown by the re-establishment of chattel slav-
ery in Sudan. Repression of women is an absolute requirement, a practice
most dramatically on display in Afghanistan, where they have been excluded from schools and jobs.

An Islamist state is, almost by definition, a rogue state, not playing by
any rules except those of expediency and power, a ruthless institution
that causes misery at home and abroad. Islamists in power means that

conflicts proliferate, society is militarized, arsenals grow, and terrorism becomes an instrument of state. It is no accident that Iran was engaged in the longest conventional war of the twentieth century (1980–88, against Iraq) and that both Sudan and Afghanistan are in the throes of decades-long civil wars, with no end in sight. Islamists repress moderate Muslims and treat non-Muslims as inferior specimens. Its apologists like to see in Islamism a force for democracy, but this ignores the key pattern that, as Martin Kramer points out, "Islamists are more likely to reach less militant positions because of their exclusion from power. . . . Weakness moderates Islamists." Power has the opposite effect.

Islamism has now been on the ascendant for more than a quarter century. Its many successes should not be understood, however, as evidence that it has widespread support. A reasonable estimate might find 10 percent of Muslims following the Islamist approach. Instead, the power that Islamists wield reflects their status as a highly dedicated, capable and well-organized minority. A little bit like cadres of the Communist Party, they make up for numbers with activism and purpose.

Islamists espouse deep antagonism toward non-Muslims in general, and Jews and Christians in particular. They despise the West both because of its huge cultural influence and because it is a traditional opponent—the old rival, Christendom, in a new guise. Some of them have learned to moderate their views so as not to upset Western audiences, but the disguise is thin and should deceive no one.

2

Islam Is Compatible with Democracy

Geneive Abdo

Geneive Abdo is the correspondent in Iran for the British newspaper the Guardian *and the author of the book* No God but God: Egypt and the Triumph of Islam.

Today's Islamic movements are less militant than past Islamic movements, such as that under Iran's Ayatollah Khomeini, which enforced strict adherence to the tenets of the Koran, the Islamic holy book. Citizens of Muslim countries are demanding more political power and choice of leadership, but at the same time they demand an Islamic rather than a secular government. Many Muslims adamantly reject Western-style democracy because it is incompatible with their concept of a religious society. In response, leaders such as Iranian president Mohammad Khatami are fusing a religious government with modern concepts of freedom to create a uniquely Islamic style of democracy.

"Those intellectuals who say that the clergy should leave politics and go back to the mosque speak on behalf of Satan," Ayatollah Ruhollah Khomeini said in 1979. So began the modern world's first experiment in establishing a religious government armed with clerics who claimed to have divine right over all temporal authorities. Now, 20 years later, Iran is refining the once-stated aims of the Iranian revolution and taking significant steps toward realizing an Islamic republic—a government that is Islamic but one in which the people have the ultimate say in matters of state.

"Democracy," considered a heretical concept in the early days of the revolution, now is embraced by the leader of the reformist movement, President Mohammad Khatami. A cleric and intellectual, Khatami believes that a religious government should serve the people's desires. "Government, although of religious character, is a human institution, and thus should be accountable to the people. In this respect, democracy may not be all that incompatible with religion," he said in a landmark newspaper interview in March 2000.

The decline of militant Islam

Western skeptics and Iran's secular elite dismiss such notions, arguing that authoritarian practices are inherent in an Islamic state, making democratic rule impossible. But in recent years, overwhelming evidence suggests the contrary, not only in Iran but in many Islamic countries. Militant Islam, which saw the rise of violent groups such as the Gamaa al-Islamiyya in Egypt, the Islamic Group in Algeria and Hamas in the Gaza Strip, now has lost its luster and has been replaced by quietest movements aiming to address the social, religious and political needs of Islamic societies.

In Egypt, a generation of moderate Islamists transformed professional unions representing hundreds of thousands of doctors, lawyers and engineers into bastions of democracy in the 1990s. For the first time, free and fair elections were held in Egypt, where President Hosni Mubarak's government upholds its monopoly on power by banning nearly all opposition parties and most newspapers. Widespread fraud has existed in parliamentary and presidential elections for two decades, allowing Mubarak to claim 96 to 99 percent of the vote in presidential polls and to exclude powerful alternative voices from the parliament. When potential Islamist candidates have appeared to gain popularity ahead of elections, the state has imprisoned them to deprive them of victory at the ballot box.

In officially secular Turkey, Necmettin Erbakan became the first Islamist prime minister in the summer of 1996—only to be ousted in June 1997, when the army threatened a coup d'etat against his government and banned his Welfare Party. In Indonesia, the world's most populous Muslim country, the new president is a moderate Islamist.

Critics point to the most extreme examples of Islamic rule in Saudi Arabia and Afghanistan to support the argument that democracy is incompatible with Islam. But there are fallacies in this assumption: In Saudi Arabia, it is a ruling feudal family, not Islamic principles, governing the country. And the Taliban's repressive and authoritarian tactics in Afghanistan hardly are considered a model by Islamic states. Iran has been at the forefront of denouncing the Taliban's distorted interpretation of the religious texts—from where it claims to justify its actions—as "un-Islamic."

Bridging the gap between Islam and democracy

Just as Iran introduced the world to the prospect of a theocracy 20 years ago, it now is at the vanguard of fusing Islam with democracy. The freest elections in the history of the Islamic republic were held in February 2000. Thousands of candidates of many political stripes competed for 290 seats in the national parliament. The election was by no means a perfect democratic exercise. The Guardian Council, an election supervisory board comprised of six conservative clerics and six jurists, did its best before and after the poll to minimize the reformists' gains. The council disqualified some candidates deemed to fall short of the proper Islamic credentials before the election and cancelled some winners after the poll.

The council even went so far as to try to hand a seat to its favorite son, former president Akbar Hashemi Rafsanjani, who appeared to have lost in the first round of voting. But when the public outcry become too intense, Rafsanjani virtually admitted defeat and tacitly acknowledged he had been granted a seat through vote-rigging on his behalf. He resigned in disgrace. That left the new parliament, primarily in the hands of reformers, a bit less hindered in what are certain to be attempts to pass progressive legislation.

Such an admission, prompted by the public's demand for fair elections, would have seemed inconceivable even a few years ago. But now, the Guardian Council, a body some would argue is a major stumbling block toward Iran's modern political development, has been forced to surrender to the public will. The Guardians say they receive their mandate from the Iranian constitution drafted after the revolution.

Clerics who wrote the document, however, say that the Guardians never were meant to run elections but only to supervise them. Ayatollah Ali Hossein Montazeri, who was Khomeini's designated successor until he fell from grace in 1989, scolds the Guardians for extending the power granted them in the constitution. Montazeri says that when he and others created the constitution they intended to establish a thriving republic where the power of the people was supreme. It is the hard-liners, he argues, who have sidetracked the process for much of the last 20 years. Only since Khatami came to power three years ago have Iran's social democrats been able to return to their aim of making a religious government democratic.

Militant Islam . . . now has lost its luster.

But how could this work in practice when such powerful bodies as the Guardian Council remain in place? Reformist clerics respond by saying the Guardians are appointed by Iran's supreme leader, who is elected by the Assembly of Experts—another clerical body—which in turn is elected directly by the people. The supreme leader, they argue, derives popular legitimacy through this process of indirect election.

This is democracy Iranian style. It certainly is non-Western, but that is the point. Iranians have no intention of creating a Westernized political system, for this would never be compatible with their notion of a religious society. Democracy does not require citizens to abandon their convictions, secularize their creed and lose faith in divine protection, argues Abdolkarim Soroush, an Iranian intellectual who is a close confidant of Khatami but who is condemned by many establishment clerics. "Embracing a faith is not contrary to freedom of choice," he writes. Conversely, Soroush argues that Islam and democracy are compatible because justice is inherent in Islam as it is in a democracy.

A long road ahead

It is apparent that Iran has a long way to go before its institutions truly are reflective of public will. The constitution must be reinterpreted; the judiciary, now under the control of conservatives, must become truly independent; and the progressive press, much of which was forcibly shut down in April 2000 upon orders from conservatives in the judiciary, must be allowed to flourish again.

Most importantly, Iran must come to terms with the institution of the supreme clerical leader, the *velayat-e faqih,* or literally "the guardianship of the supreme juriconsult." While the general concept has solid roots in Shiite Islam, Khomeini revolutionized the practice to establish clerical power over republican rule. Defining the *velayat's* role is critical to the degree to which Iran will become a democratic religious government. The supreme leader controls the armed forces, the judiciary and the state-run TV network and even has final say over the election of the president.

Khomeini believed that the *velayat* had divine powers from God which should not be challenged by the people. As a great theologian and master politician, only he could fulfill this role. More than a decade after his death, it is evident that the concept must be altered if it is going to survive.

In today's Iran, there is a public outcry for more democracy and less interference by the clerics in politics. There were fewer clerics elected to the parliament in February 2000 than at any other time since the revolution. But this growing anticlerical sentiment has been misinterpreted by the outside world. Iran's youth are at the forefront of public criticism, but their complaints are by no means against Islam. They simply are tired of the establishment's strict interpretation of religion infringing upon their private lives. Young people want more flexibility in Islam and a new reading of the faith that would be more relevant to modern times.

A broad spectrum of clerics in the holy Shiite city of Qom are heeding this public demand for a modern interpretation of Islam. Religious opinions are being issued to address contemporary social issues unforeseen by early Shiite theologians. Seminary education has been expanded to include a broad range of subjects to prepare budding clerics for modernity.

All of these changes, fueled by the increasing political power of the public, are occurring within an Islamic framework of government. There may never come a day when Iran's supreme leader is elected directly by the people or the institution is abolished entirely. While that may be the West's ultimate test for an Iranian democracy, such thinking misses the point. Iran is struggling to carve out a political system which is both "democratic" and Islamic at the same time. If the Islamic Republic succeeds, it could provide a model for other Muslim states—a prospect that certainly would be in the interest of the United States.

3

Fundamentalist Islam Is Not Compatible with Democracy

Ausaf Ali

Ausaf Ali is a former professor at the Graduate School of Business Administration at the University of Karachi and the author of Broader Dimensions of the Ideology of Pakistan.

Muslims, particularly Pakistani Muslims, have failed at creating lasting democratic governments. Islamic fundamentalists do not appreciate the dynamism and rationality that are necessary to maintain a democratic government, mainly because Islam does not champion these values. According to Islamic tradition, the Prophet Muhammad ruled according to Allah's (God's) will, and the consent of the governed was irrelevant to his rule. Moreover, Islam and democracy are incompatible because Muslims reject diversity, the acceptance of which is essential to a successful democracy.

It has been well said that those who do not learn from history are condemned to repeat it. I offer Pakistan as a case in point. In its 52 years of history, Pakistan—created on August 14, 1947, out of British India, which became independent a day later—has been placed under military rule after the overthrow of the civilian government by the Pakistani army in 1958, 1977 and 1999. Even during civilian rule, the army has called the shots from behind the elected leaders of Pakistan. While India is the most populous democracy in the world, Pakistan has miserably failed at any kind of democracy, including Islamic. It is clear that along with democracy, all the Islamization programs have failed. Islam and the Sharia, or Islamic law, simply do not have the conceptual resources, flexibility and dynamism to suffice for the governance of a modern state and operation of a rational economy and an expanding civil society. By now, Pakistanis have developed a sad conviction that democracy as we know it is just not a workable form of government for their country, because Pakistanis do not have the social psychology, the political culture, the social ethics or the common decency for making democracy work.

Ideological differences

The difference in the fortunes of democracy in India and Pakistan is that the world view of Indians is derived from Hinduism and that of Pakistanis from Islam. Ideologically, Hinduism is quite compatible with secularism, democracy and democratic values. Islam is hostile toward all three. As the founder and chief executive of the first Islamic polity at Medina in what is today Saudi Arabia, Muhammad ruled in accordance with the will of Allah as revealed to him and translated into his own will. Nothing could have been more irrelevant to his rule than the consent of the governed. There was no room for "we the people" or for legislation by elected representatives of the people because the whole body of laws as laid down in the Sharia was valid and binding for all times. That is the reason why parliaments in Muslim countries even today are rubber-stamp bodies. Neither citizens' right to criticize nor to dissent from their rulers are recognized. Islam admonishes Muslims to obey Allah, his prophet and those in power, as it admonishes women to obey men, because "men are a degree above them."

Muhammad ruled in accordance with the will of Allah as revealed to him and translated into his own will.

Islam puts women, minorities and nonconformists at a disadvantage. Muslims do not recognize the idea of diversity in their own countries, though they take the fullest advantage of it in the West. To be sure, a woman rose to the position of the prime minister in Pakistan, but this was resented by fundamentalist Muslim men, because Muhammad prophesied that any nation or organization with a woman as its leader is headed for disaster. Non-Muslims, heretics, apostates and homosexuals are regarded as fit for persecution.

Given the attitudes Islam imparts to Muslims, it is apparent why democracy failed in Pakistan: because fundamentalist Islam and democracy are not compatible. Once this is realized, an honest search for a suitable form of political system, even if less satisfactory than democracy, can begin. As a Pakistani, I find it sad that a people who can master the rules of cricket should have failed so miserably at learning the rules of democracy, which are far simpler. So long as Pakistanis insist on applying the uncompromising demands of fundamentalist Islam, democracy has no chance in Pakistan. Sadly, democracy seems to be doomed in the foreseeable future in the whole world of Islam.

Islamist Misogyny Has Its Roots in Islam

Ibn Warraq

Ibn Warraq, who was raised a Muslim, now devotes himself to the scholarly examination of the beliefs and practices of Islam. He is the author of The Origins of the Koran, The Quest for Historical Muhammad, What the Koran Really Says: Language, Text, and Commentary, *and* Why I Am Not a Muslim.

Women in many Islamic societies lack basic human rights, independent legal status, and the right to support themselves. Many Muslim women also suffer physical abuse such as public beatings and rape from their husbands, families, and authorities. Muslims who practice these and other abuses justify their actions by pointing to passages in the Koran that deem men superior to women. The Koran also sanctifies beating disobedient wives and "honor killings"—murdering female family members for suspected adultery or fornication. Even though these misogynist beliefs are inculcated by Islam, many Muslim women are speaking out against such abuses and forming organizations to fight for women's rights in Muslim nations.

Islam is deeply anti-woman. Islam is the fundamental cause of the repression of Muslim women and remains the major obstacle to the evolution of their position. Islam has always considered women as creatures inferior in every way: physically, intellectually, and morally. This negative vision is divinely sanctioned in the Koran, corroborated by the *hadiths* [reports of Muhammad's sayings or actions], and perpetuated by the commentaries of the theologians, the custodians of Muslim dogma and ignorance.

Far better for these intellectuals to abandon the religious argument, to reject these sacred texts, and have recourse to *reason* alone. They should turn instead to human rights. The Universal Declaration of Human Rights (adopted on December 10, 1948, by the General Assembly of the United Nations in Paris and ratified by most Muslim countries) at no point has recourse to a religious argument. These rights are based on natural rights, which any adult human being capable of choice has. They are rights that human beings have simply because they are human beings. Human reason or rationality is the ultimate arbiter of rights—human rights, the rights of women.

Unfortunately, in practice, in Muslim countries one cannot simply leave the theologians with their narrow, bigoted world view to themselves. One cannot ignore the *ulama*, those learned doctors of Muslim law who by their *fatwas* or decisions in questions touching private or public matters of importance regulate the life of the Muslim community. They still exercise considerable powers of approving or forbidding certain actions. Why the continuing influence of the *mullas* [conservative religious leaders]?

The Koran remains for all Muslims, not just "fundamentalists," the uncreated word of God Himself. It is valid for all times and places; its ideas are absolutely true and beyond all criticism. To question it is to question the very word of God, and hence blasphemous. A Muslim's duty is to believe it and obey its divine commands.

Islam is the fundamental cause of the repression of Muslim women.

Several other factors contribute to the continuing influence of the *ulama*. Any religion that requires total obedience without thought is not likely to produce people capable of *critical thought*, people capable of free and independent thought. Such a situation is favorable to the development of a powerful "clergy" and is clearly responsible for the intellectual, cultural, and economic stagnation of several centuries. Illiteracy remains high in Muslim countries. Historically, as there never was any separation of state and religion, any criticism of one was seen as a criticism of the other. Inevitably, when many Muslim countries won independence after the Second World War, Islam was unfortunately linked with nationalism, which meant that any criticism of Islam was seen as a betrayal of the newly independent country—an unpatriotic act, an encouragement to colonialism and imperialism. No Muslim country has developed a stable democracy; Muslims are being subjected to every kind of repression possible. Under these conditions healthy criticism of society is not possible, because critical thought and liberty go together.

The above factors explain why Islam in general and the position of women in particular are never criticized, discussed, or subjected to deep scientific or skeptical analysis. All innovations are discouraged in Islam—every problem is seen as a religious problem rather than a social or economic one.

Profoundly anti-woman

Islam took the legend of Adam and Eve from the Old Testament and adapted it in its own fashion. The creation of mankind from one person is mentioned in the following *suras*:

> 4.1. O Mankind! Be careful of your duty to your Lord who created you from a single soul and from it created its mate

and from them twain hath spread abroad a multiple of men and women.

39.6. He created you from one being, then from that (being) He made its mate.

7.189. He it is who did create you from a single soul and therefrom did make his mate that he might take rest in her.

From these slender sources Muslim theologians have concluded that man was the original creation—womankind was created secondarily for the pleasure and repose of man. The legend was further developed to re-inforce the supposed inferiority of women. Finally, the legend was given a sacred character so that to criticize it was to criticize the very words of God, which were immutable and absolute. Here is how Muhammad describes women in general: "Be friendly to women for womankind was created from a rib, but the bent part of the rib, high up, if you try to straighten it you will break it; if you do nothing, she will continue to be bent."

God punishes Adam and Eve for disobeying his orders. But there is nothing in the verses to show that it was Eve (as in the Old Testament) who led Adam astray. And yet Muslim exegetists and jurists have created the myth of Eve the temptress that has since become an integral part of Muslim tradition. Muhammad himself is reputed to have said: "If it had not been for Eve, no woman would have been unfaithful to her husband."

Muslim theologians have concluded that man was the original creation [and] womankind was created secondarily.

The Islamic tradition also attributes guile and deceit to women and draws its support from the Koran. Modern Muslim commentators inter-pret certain verses to show that guile, deceit, and treachery are intrinsic to a woman's nature. Not only is she unwilling to change, she is by na-ture incapable of changing—she has no choice. In attacking the female deities of the polytheists, the Koran takes the opportunity to malign the female sex further.

4.1 17. They invoke in His stead only females; they pray to none else than Satan, a rebel.

53.21–22. Are yours the males and His the females? That in-deed were an unfair division!

53.27. Lo! it is those who disbelieve in the Hereafter who name the angels with the names of females.

Other verses from the Koran also seem of a misogynist tendency.

2.228. Women who are divorced shall wait, keeping them-selves apart, three (monthly) courses. And it is not lawful for them that they should conceal that which Allah hath created in their wombs if they are believers in Allah and the Last Day. And their husbands would do better to take them back in that case if they desire a reconciliation. And they (women) have rights similar to those (of men) over them in kindness, and men are a degree above them. Allah is Mighty, Wise.

2.282. But if he who oweth the debt is of low understanding, or weak or unable himself to dictate, then let the guardian of his interests dictate in (terms of) equity. And call to witness, from among your men, two witnesses. And if two men be not (at hand) then a man and two women, of such as ye approve as witnesses, so that if the one erreth (through forgetfulness) the other will remember.

4.11. Allah chargeth you concerning (the provision for) your children: to the male the equivalent of the portion of two females.

4.34. Men are in charge of women, because Allah hath made the one of them to excel the other, and because they spend of their property (for the support of women). So good women are the obedient, guarding in secret that which Allah hath guarded. As for those from whom ye fear rebellion, admonish them and banish them to beds apart; and scourge (beat) them. Then if they obey you, seek not a way against them Lo! Allah is ever High Exalted, Great.

Equally, in numerous *hadiths* on which are based the Islamic laws, we learn of the woman's role—to stay at home, to be at the beck and call of man, to obey him (which is a religious duty), and to assure man a tranquil existence. Here are some examples of these traditions:

- The woman who dies and with whom the husband is satisfied will go to paradise.
- A wife should never refuse herself to her husband even if it is on the saddle of a camel.
- Hellfire appeared to me in a dream and I noticed that it was above all peopled with women who had been ungrateful. "Was it toward God that they were ungrateful?" They had not shown any gratitude toward their husbands for all they had received from them. Even when all your life you have showered a woman with your largesse she will still find something petty to reproach you with one day, saying, "You have never done anything for me."
- If anything presages a bad omen it is: a house, a woman, a horse.
- Never will a people know success if they confide their affairs to a woman.

It will be appropriate to include two quotes from the famous and much revered philosopher al-Ghazali (1058–1111), whom Professor Montgomery Watt describes as the greatest Muslim after Muhammad. In his "The Revival Of The Religious Sciences," Ghazali defines the woman's role:

She should stay at home and get on with her spinning, she should not go out often, she must not be well-informed, nor must she be communicative with her neighbours and only visit them when absolutely necessary; she should take care of her husband and respect him in his presence and his absence and seek to satisfy him in everything; she must not cheat on him nor extort money from him; she must not leave her house without his permission and if given his permission she must leave surreptitiously. She should put on old clothes and take deserted streets and alleys, avoid markets, and make sure that a stranger does not hear her voice or recognize her; she must not speak to a friend of her husband even in need. . . . Her sole worry should be her virtue, her home as well as her prayers and her fast. If a friend of her husband calls when the latter is absent she must not open the door nor reply to him in order to safeguard her and her husband's honour. She should accept what her husband gives her as sufficient sexual needs at any moment. . . . She should be clean and ready to satisfy her husband's sexual needs at any moment.

Such are some of the sayings from the putative golden age of Islamic feminism. It was claimed that it was the abandonment of the original teachings of Islam that had led to the present decadence and backwardness of Muslim societies. But there never was an Islamic utopia. To talk of a golden age is only to conform and perpetuate the influence of the clergy, the mullas, and their hateful creed that denies humanity to half the inhabitants of this globe, and further retards all serious attempts to liberate Muslim women.

What rights?

The inequality between men and women in matters of giving testimony or evidence or being a witness is enshrined in the Koran: *Sura* 2.282 (quoted above).

How do Muslim apologists justify the above text? Muslim men and women writers point to the putative psychological differences that exist between men and women. The Koran (and hence God) in its sublime wisdom knew that women are sensitive, emotional, sentimental, easily moved, and influenced by their biological rhythm, lacking judgment. But above all they have a shaky memory. In other words, women are psychologically inferior. Such are the dubious arguments used by Muslim intellectuals—male and, astonishingly enough, female intellectuals like Ahmad Jamal, Ms. Zahya Kaddoura, Ms. Ghada al-Kharsa, and Ms. Madiha Khamis. As [Islamic scholar] Ghassan Ascha [in his book *Du statut Inferieur de la Femme en Islam*] points out, the absurdity of their arguments are obvious.

By taking the testimony of two beings whose reasoning faculties are faulty we do not obtain the testimony of one complete person with a perfectly functioning rational faculty—such is Islamic arithmetic! By this logic, if the testimony of two women is worth that of one man, then the testimony of four women must be worth that of two men, in which case we can dispense with the testimony of the men. But no! In Islam the rule is not to accept the testimony of women alone in matters to which men theoretically have access. It is said that the Prophet did not accept the testimony of women in matters of marriage, divorce, and *hudud. Hudud* are the punishments set down by Muhammad in the Koran and the *hadith* for (1) adultery—stoning to death; (2) fornication—a hundred stripes; (3) false accusation of adultery against a married person—eighty stripes; (4) apostasy—death; (5) drinking wine—eighty stripes; (6) theft—the cutting off of the right hand; (7) simple robbery on the highway—the loss of hands and feet; robbery with murder—death, either by the sword or by crucifixion.

On adultery the Koran 24.4 says: "Those that defame honourable women and cannot produce four witnesses shall be given eighty lashes." Of course, Muslim jurists will only accept four male witnesses. These witnesses must declare that they have "seen the parties in the very act of carnal conjunction." Once an accusation of fornication and adultery has been made, the accuser himself or herself risks punishment if he or she does not furnish the necessary legal proofs. Witnesses are in the same situation. If a man were to break into a woman's dormitory and rape half a dozen women, he would risk nothing since there would be no male witnesses. Indeed the victim of a rape would hesitate before going in front of the law, since she would risk being condemned herself and have little chance of obtaining justice. "If the woman's words were sufficient in such cases," explains Judge Zharoor ul Haq of Pakistan, "then no man would be safe." This iniquitous situation is truly revolting and yet for Muslim law it is a way of avoiding social scandal concerning the all-important sexual taboo. Women found guilty of fornication were literally immured, at first; as the Koran 4.15 says: "Shut them up within their houses till death release them, or God make some way for them." However this was later canceled and stoning substituted for adultery and one hundred lashes for fornication. When a man is to be stoned to death, he is taken to some barren place, where he is stoned first by the witnesses, then the judge, and then the public. When a woman is stoned, a hole to receive her is dug as deep as her waist—the Prophet himself seems to have ordered such procedure. It is lawful for a man to kill his wife and her lover if he catches them in the very act.

The woman's role [is] to stay at home, to be at the beck and call of man, to obey him . . . and to assure man a tranquil existence.

In the case where a man suspects his wife of adultery or denies the legitimacy of the offspring, his testimony is worth that of four men. *Sura* 24.6: "If a man accuses his wife but has no witnesses except himself, he shall swear four times by God that his charge is true, calling down upon himself the curse of God if he is lying. But if his wife swears four times by God that his charge is false and calls down His curse upon herself if it be true, she shall receive no punishment." Appearances to the contrary, this is not an example of Koranic justice or equality between the sexes. The woman indeed escapes being stoned to death but she remains rejected and loses her right to the dowry and her right to maintenance, *whatever the outcome of the trial.* A woman does not have the right to charge her husband in a similar manner. Finally, for a Muslim marriage to be valid there must be a multiplicity of witnesses. For Muslim jurists, two men form a multiplicity but not two or three or a thousand women.

Muslim inheritance

In questions of heritage, the Koran tells us that male children should inherit twice the portion of female children:

> 4.11–12. A male shall inherit twice as much as a female. If there be more than two girls, they shall have two-thirds of the inheritance, but if there be one only, she shall inherit the half. Parents shall inherit a sixth each, if the deceased have a child; but if he leave no child and his parents be his heirs, his mother shall have a third. If he have brothers, his mother shall have a sixth after payment of any legacy he may have bequeathed or any debt he may have owed.

To justify this inequality, Muslim authors lean heavily on the fact that a woman receives a dowry and has the right to maintenance from her husband. It is also true that according to Muslim law the mother is not at all obliged to provide for her children, and if she does spend money on her children, it is, to quote G.H. Bousquet [in his book *L'Ethique Sexuelle de L'Islam*], "recoverable by her from her husband if he is returned to a better fortune as in the case of any other charitable person. Therefore there is no point in the husband and wife sharing in the taking charge of the household; this weighs upon the husband alone. There is no longer any financial interest between them."

This latter point referred to by Bousquet simply emphasizes the negative aspects of a Muslim marriage—that is to say, the total absence of any idea of "association" between "couples" as in Christianity. As to dowry, it is, of course, simply a reconfirmation of the man's claims over the woman in matters of sex and divorce. Furthermore, in reality the woman does not get to use the dowry for herself. The custom is either to use the dowry to furnish the house of the newly married couple or for the wife to offer it to her father. According to the Malekites [Christian Byzantines], the woman can be obliged by law to use the dowry to furnish the house. Muslim law also gives the guardian the right to cancel a marriage—even that of a woman of legal age—if he thinks the dowry is not sufficient. Thus the dowry, instead of being a sign of her independence, turns out once more to be a symbol of her servitude.

The woman has the right to maintenance but this simply emphasizes her total dependence on her husband, with all its attendant sense of insecurity. According to Muslim jurists, the husband is not obliged under Islamic law to pay for her medical expenses in case of illness. Financial independence of the woman would of course be the first step in the liberation of Muslim women and thus it is not surprising that it is seen as a threat to male dominance. Muslim women are now obliged to take equal responsibility for looking after their parents. Article 158 of Syrian law states "The child—male or female—having the necessary means is obliged to take responsibility for his or her poor parents." The birth of a girl is still seen as a catastrophe in Islamic societies. The system of inheritance just adds to her misery and her dependence on the man. If she is an only child she receives only half the legacy of her father; the other half goes to the male members of the father's family. If there are two or more daughters, they inherit two-thirds. This pushes fathers and mothers to prefer male children to female so that they can leave the entirety of their effects or possessions to their own descendants. "Yet when a new-born girl is announced to one of them his countenance darkens and he is filled with gloom" (*sura* 43.15). The situation is even worse when a woman loses her husband—she only receives a quarter of the legacy. If the deceased leaves more than one wife, all the wives are still obliged to share among themselves a quarter or one-eighth of the legacy.

In Islam the rule is not to accept the testimony of women alone in matters to which men theoretically have access.

Muslim jurists are unanimous in their view that men are superior to women in virtue of their reasoning abilities, their knowledge, and their supervisory powers. And since it is the man who assumes financial responsibility for the family, it is argued, it is natural that he should have total power over the woman. These same jurists, of course, totally neglect changing social conditions where a woman may contribute her salary to the upkeep of her family—power over women remains a divine command and "natural" or "in the nature of things." Muslim thinkers continue to confine Muslim women to the house—to leave the house is against the will of God and against the principles of Islam. Confined to their houses, women are then reproached for not having any experience of the outside world!

According to theologians, the husband has the right to administer corporal punishment to his wife if she

1. Refuses to make herself beautiful for him;
2. Refuses to meet his sexual demands;
3. Leaves the house without permission or without any legitimate reason recognized by law; or
4. Neglects her religious duties.

A *hadith* attributes the following saying to the Prophet: "Hang up your whip where your wife can see it." There are a number of other *hadiths* that contradict this one. In those, Muhammad explicitly forbids men to beat their wives—in which case the Prophet himself is contradicting what the Koran, enshrining divine law, permits.

Case histories: The women of Pakistan

In Pakistan in 1977, General Zia al-Haq took over in a military coup declaring that the process of Islamization was not going fast enough. The *mullas* had finally got someone who was prepared to listen to them.

Zia imposed martial law, total press censorship, and began creating a theocratic state, believing that Pakistan ought to have "the spirit of Islam." He banned women from athletic contests and even enforced the Muslim fast during the month of Ramadan at gunpoint. He openly admitted that there was a contradiction between Islam and democracy. Zia introduced Islamic laws that discriminated against women. The most notorious of these laws were the *Zina* and *Hudud* Ordinances that called for the Islamic punishments of the amputation of hands for stealing and stoning to death for married people found guilty of illicit sex. The term *zina* included adultery, fornication, and rape, and even prostitution. Fornication was punished with a maximum of a hundred lashes administered in public and ten years' imprisonment.

In practice, these laws protect rapists, for a woman who has been raped often finds herself charged with adultery or fornication. To prove *zina*, four Muslim adult males of good repute must be present to testify that sexual penetration has taken place. Furthermore, in keeping with good Islamic practice, these laws value the testimony of men over women. The combined effect of these laws is that it is impossible for a woman to bring a successful charge of rape against a man; instead, she herself, the victim, finds herself charged with illicit sexual intercourse, while the rapist goes free. If the rape results in a pregnancy, this is automatically taken as an admission that adultery or fornication has taken place with the woman's consent rather than that rape has occurred.

Here are some sample cases.

In a town in the northern province of Punjab, a woman and her two daughters were stripped naked, beaten, and gangraped in public, but the police declined to pursue the case.

A thirteen-year-old girl was kidnapped and raped by a "family friend." When her father brought a case against the rapist, it was the girl who was put in prison and charged with *zina*, illegal sexual intercourse. The father managed to secure the child's release by bribing the police. The traumatized child was then severely beaten for disgracing the family honor.

The birth of a girl is still seen as a catastrophe in Islamic societies.

A fifty-year-old widow, Ahmedi Begum, decided to let some rooms in her house in the city of Lahore to two young veiled women. As she was about to show them the rooms, the police burst into the courtyard of the house and arrested the two girls and Ahmedi Begum's nephew, who had simply been standing there. Later that afternoon, Ahmedi Begum went to the police station with her son-in-law to inquire about her nephew and the two girls. The police told Ahmedi they were arresting her too. They confiscated her jewelry and pushed her into another room. While she was waiting, the police officers shoved the two girls, naked and bleeding, into the room and then proceeded to rape them again in front of the widow. When Ahmedi covered her eyes, the police forced her to watch by pulling her arms to her sides. After suffering various sexual humiliations, Ahmedi herself was stripped and raped by one officer after another. They dragged her outside where she was again beaten. One of the officers forced a policeman's truncheon, covered with chili paste, into her rectum, rupturing it. Ahmedi screamed in horrible agony and fainted, only to wake up in prison, charged with *zina*. Her case was taken up by a human rights lawyer. She was released on bail after three months in prison, but was not acquitted until three years later. In the meantime, her son-in-law divorced her daughter because of his shame.

A woman who has been raped often finds herself charged with adultery or fornication.

Was this an isolated case? Unfortunately no. The Human Rights Commission of Pakistan said in its annual report that one woman is raped every three hours in Pakistan and one in two rape victims is a juvenile. According to Women's Action Forum, a woman's rights organization, 72% of all women in police custody in Pakistan are physically and sexually abused. Furthermore, 75% of all women in jail are there under charges of *zina*. Many of these women remain in jail awaiting trial for years.

In other words, the charge of *zina* is casually applied by any man who wants to get rid of his wife, who is immediately arrested, and kept waiting in prison, sometimes for years. Before the introduction of these laws the total number of women in prison was 70; the 1995 number was more than 3,000. Most of these women have been charged under the *Zina* or *Hudud* Ordinances.

Muslim women in politics

The Western press naively believed that the election of Benazir Bhutto as Pakistan's prime minister in November 1988 would revolutionize women's role not just in Pakistan, but in the entire Islamic world. Under Islamic law of course, women cannot be head of an Islamic state, and Pakistan had become an Islamic republic under the new constitution of 1956. Thus, Benazir Bhutto had defied the *mullas* and won. But her government lasted a bare 20 months, during which period Nawaz Sharif, who was the prime minister briefly in the early 1990s, is said to have encouraged the *mullas* in their opposition to having a woman as the head of an Islamic state. Benazir Bhutto's government was dismissed on charges of corruption, and her husband imprisoned in 1990.

The lot of the Muslim woman was harsh before Benazir's election, and nothing has changed. She has pandered to the religious lobby, the mullas, the very people who insist that a woman cannot hold power in an Islamic state, and has repeatedly postponed any positive action on the position of women.

Pakistan shows the same grim picture. Pakistan is one of only four countries in the world where female life expectancy (51 years) is lower than the male (52 years); the average female life expectancy for all poor countries is 61 years. A large number of Pakistani women die in pregnancy or childbirth, six for every 1,000 live births. Despite the fact that contraception has never been banned by orthodox Islam, under Zia the Islamic Ideology Council of Pakistan declared family planning to be un-Islamic. Various *mullas* condemned family planning as a Western conspiracy to emasculate Islam. As a result, the average fertility rate per woman in Pakistan is 6.9. Pakistan is also among the world's bottom ten countries for female attendance at primary schools. Some people put female literacy in the rural areas as low as 2% *(Economist*, March 5, 1994). As the *Economist* put it, "Some of the blame for all this lies with the attempt of the late President Zia ul Haq to create an Islamic republic. . . . Zia turned the clock back. A 1984 law of his, for instance, gives a woman's legal evidence half the weight of a man's" *(Economist*, January 13, 1990).

Indeed a large part of the blame lies with the attitudes inculcated by Islam, which has always seen woman as inferior to man. The birth of a baby girl is the occasion for mourning. Hundreds of baby girls are abandoned every year in the gutters and dust bins and on the pavements. An organization working in Karachi to save these children has calculated that more than five hundred children are abandoned a year in Karachi alone, and that 99% of them are girls.

Little did Jinnah, the founder of Pakistan, realize how literally true his words were when he said in a 1944 speech: "No nation can rise to the height of glory unless your women are side by side with you. We are victims of evil customs. It is a crime against humanity that our women are shut up within the four walls of the houses as prisoners."

But we do not need to leave with a completely pessimistic picture. Pakistani women have shown themselves to be very courageous, and more and more are fighting for their rights with the help of equally brave organizations such as Women's Action Forum (WAF) and War Against Rape. WAF was formed in 1981 as women came onto the streets to protest against the *Hudud* Ordinances, and to demonstrate their solidarity with a couple who had recently been sentenced to death by stoning for fornication. In 1983, women organized the first demonstrations against martial law.

5

Islamist Misogyny Does Not Have Its Roots in Islam

Teresa Watanabe

Teresa Watanabe, winner of the James O. Supple Contest for Religion Writer of the Year in 2000, is a religion writer for the Los Angeles Times.

Many women suffer human rights abuses in Muslim countries—in Afghanistan women are denied jobs and education, and in Saudi Arabia women are forbidden to drive—but the misogyny stems from cultural factors rather than from Islam. In fact, the Koran advocates equality of the sexes and humanitarian treatment of women. Men who violate women's rights in Muslim countries misinterpret the egalitarian teachings of the Koran.

It seems a paradox: Muslim women are denied jobs and schooling in Afghanistan, cannot drive in Saudi Arabia and are murdered by relatives for suspected sexual indiscretions in "honor killings" in places ranging from Jordan to Pakistan. But a group of Muslim women at a Koranic recitation class in Pasadena, California, unanimously declares that Islam upholds perfect gender equality.

Why?

Because the word of God as revealed in verse after verse of the Koran and in the traditions of the Prophet Muhammad consistently lays out egalitarian teachings, these women say. They are a diverse group of Americans with heritages ranging from African and Palestinian to Egyptian, Sri Lankan and Irish, some sporting sweaters and slacks and others brilliantly colored robes and head coverings.

The Koran gives women a list of specifically enumerated rights, from inheritance to divorce, that were startling advances at the time they were conveyed 1,400 years ago. But, the women say, fallible practices of men have consistently skewed the word and ignored women's God-given rights in order to prop up patriarchal cultures and repressive political regimes.

"Sometimes the relation between culture and religion gets so melded, it's hard to tease it out and see which is which," said Laila Al-Marayati, a Glendale, California, gynecologist whose Muslim Women's League sponsored the class on the beautiful but breathtakingly difficult art of Koranic recitation—an art traditionally less accessible to women than men.

The 1999 funeral of King Hussein of Jordan highlighted the confusion over women's status in Islam, which many Muslims say is one of the most misunderstood aspects of their religion. In one of the more noted aspects of the funeral, Queen Noor and other women were not permitted to attend, in accord with what many news reports called "Islamic tradition."

That prompted the Muslim Public Affairs Council to issue a statement that the exclusion was "a cultural tradition garbed in Islamic clothing that varies from one place to another." It noted that the fundamentalist regime of Iran did not bar women from funerals and that several women witnessed the burial of the prophet, including his family members.

In other reflections of the vast diversity of Muslim practices regarding women, Egypt has no female judges but such places as Syria, Morocco, Tunisia do; women are not allowed to lead mixed gatherings in prayer in most Muslim countries but can in Indonesia, said Yvonne Haddad, a Georgetown University professor of Islamic studies.

The Koran gives women a list of specifically enumerated rights.

Albania and Bosnia don't give women any inheritance despite explicit Koranic instructions to do so, while most Muslim families ignore exhortations for chastity from both genders and expect it only from females, others say.

Saudi ban on women drivers

Many of the most repressive practices ascribed to Islam are based on cultural traditions, social considerations or contested interpretations, many Muslims say. Even Saudi-trained scholars, for instance, agree that the kingdom's ban on women driving is not grounded in the Koran or the prophet's traditions. Instead it is a modern social measure aimed at preventing women and men from mingling in unsafe or unexpected circumstances—such as a woman's car breaking down. (Recent news reports suggest the Saudis may revoke their rule because the cost of providing 500,000 imported male chauffeurs for women is taxing the shrinking royal treasury.) "Nothing in Islam prevents women from driving—the wife of the prophet rode a camel—but tradition overcame certain teachings of Islam," said Hussam Ayloush of the Council on American-Islamic Relations.

The treatment of women under the Taliban of Afghanistan is widely condemned by Islamic scholars as an affront to Islam. The fundamentalist regime has barred women from working and attending school, forced them to cover themselves from head to toe and imposed a blizzard of repressive rules, including no singing, loud laughs or wearing shoes that click lest the sounds lure men into "corruption." Reports of beatings, rape and torture are rife—and transmitted to the world via the Web site of the Revolutionary Association of the Women of Afghanistan (http://www.rawa.org).

Islamic scholars around the world have plied the Taliban with opinions that such measures drastically violate Koranic teachings of respect and equality for women; Afghan native Wais Al-Qarni was so incensed, he says, that he fired off a letter to the Afghan Embassy in Washington but never received a response.

Many of the most repressive practices ascribed to Islam are based on cultural traditions.

"They are beating women, preventing them from learning, but Allah says men and women are one," said Al-Qarni, 23, an Oakland, California, college student studying criminology.

The misuse of Islam to justify sexism has prompted the Muslim Women's League and other organizations to urge women to directly study the Koran and the prophet's traditions to gain their own understanding of the egalitarian vision laid out in them. "Our main message to women is that our religion is from God and not human beings, and don't accept any intermediaries between you and God," said Sharifa Alkhateeb of the Washington-based North American Council for Muslim Women.

The organization works to educate Muslim women and combat dismal public stereotypes that they are "controlled by men, don't think clearly, are probably battered and, if they cover their heads, can't speak English," Alkhateeb said.

Similarly, the Muslim Women's League sends out speakers, sponsors sports camps for girls, organizes Koranic study groups and issues position papers highlighting Islam's egalitarian teachings ranging from women's legal rights to their spiritual roles.

Unlike the Bible, Al-Marayati said, the Koran does not hold that Eve was made from Adam's rib or tempted him into sin; both were created equally, both erred, both were banished and both were forgiven.

The Islamic texts also sing the praises of strong and noble women, from the prophet's wife to the Queen of Sheba to Mary, the mother of Jesus, and notes that women battled in the prophet's armies, held positions of religious leadership and worked in business and commerce.

The Koran condemns female infanticide, a common practice in pre-Islamic Arabia, and details a long list of women's rights: to own property, engage in business, choose a marriage partner, divorce, claim inheritance, receive education and be treated with respect and dignity, Alkhateeb said.

Some like clothing rules

Alkhateeb and others say that many practices seen as repressive by non-Muslims are in fact liberating—such as wearing head coverings and other modest clothing.

"The main reason we wear a head covering is to set ourselves apart from males and insist they observe us as human beings, with ideas and concepts, rather than be distracted by hair and perfume and makeup,"

Alkhateeb said. Still, she said, numerous Muslim American women have been denied jobs by airlines, restaurants, even universities because of their attire.

"There is such a horrible negative image associated with the scarf: of ignorance, dirty hair or terrorism," Alkhateeb said.

Talibah Jilani of the Kamilat women's organization based in Mountain View, California, said other seemingly sexist practices should be viewed in context: Dictates for male relatives to travel with women, for instance, were made during the time of widespread war and banditry and not only protected them but also freed them from the burden of carrying luggage and the like. Even polygamy, she said, was originally sanctioned as a compassionate way to support war widows who might otherwise be forced into prostitution or poverty.

Still, Muslim women acknowledge that a great gap too often exists between Islam's ideal regarding women and their actual treatment. For instance, all three women's organizations are tackling domestic violence, as significant a problem in their community as nationwide.

In one limited study, Alkhateeb's group found about 10% of Muslim leaders reported instances of domestic violence; a more extensive national survey is currently underway. The Muslim Women's League had a conference on the issue in 1999.

"I think more women are saying we need to wake up, learn to educate ourselves, be more active in the community and have our voices heard," said Fatima Cash, a Muslim Women's League member who converted to Islam from Catholicism 22 years ago.

6

Islamic Fundamentalism Is a Threat to the United States

Daniel Pipes

Daniel Pipes is a political analyst whose articles have appeared in numerous publications including the Atlantic Monthly, Foreign Affairs, Harper's, *the* National Review, *the* New Republic, *and the* Weekly Standard. *He has also written several books, such as* The Hidden Hand: Middle East Fears of Conspiracy *and* The Long Shadow: Culture and Politics in the Middle East.

After the terrorist attacks on September 11, 2001, pundits spoke in defense of Islam and the millions of American Muslims who are not associated with terrorist groups. Although these moderate Muslims constitute the majority of Muslims in America, a small but significant faction of fundamentalist Muslims, or Islamists, conspire to take over America. These Islamists believe that triumph over America would signify dominance over liberalism and Christianity that are so valued in the West and resented in the Middle East. Some Islamists resort to violence, but most simply strive to increase the number of Muslims in America and introduce Islamic customs into American society. A hostile Islamic coup in America seems farfetched, but Islamic fundamentalists are farsighted and dedicated to their goals.

In the aftermath of the violence on September 11, 2001, American politicians from President George W. Bush on down have tripped over themselves to affirm that the vast majority of Muslims living in the United States are just ordinary people. Here is how the President put it during a visit to a mosque on September 17, 2001: "America counts millions of Muslims among our citizens, and Muslims make an incredibly valuable contribution to our country. Muslims are doctors, lawyers, law professors, members of the military, entrepreneurs, shopkeepers, moms and dads." Two days later, he added that "there are millions of good Americans who practice the Muslim faith who love their country as much as I love the country, who salute the flag as strongly as I salute the flag."

These soothing words, echoed and amplified by many columnists and editorial writers, were obviously appropriate at a moment of high national tension and amid reports of mounting bias against Muslims living in the United States. And it is certainly true that the number of militant Islamic operatives with plans to carry out terrorist attacks on the United States is statistically tiny. But the situation is more complex than the President would have it.

The Muslim population in this country is not like any other group, for it includes within it a substantial body of people—many times more numerous than the agents of Osama bin Laden who share with the suicide hijackers a hatred of the United States and the desire, ultimately, to transform it into a nation living under the strictures of militant Islam. Although not responsible for the atrocities in September 2001, they harbor designs for this country that warrant urgent and serious attention.

The militant Islamic threat

In June 1991, Siraj Wahaj, a black convert to Islam and the recipient of some of the American Muslim community's highest honors, had the privilege of becoming the first Muslim to deliver the daily prayer in the U.S. House of Representatives. On that occasion he recited from the Qur'an and appealed to the Almighty to guide American leaders "and grant them righteousness and wisdom."

A little over a year later, addressing an audience of New Jersey Muslims, the same Wahaj articulated a rather different message from his mild and moderate invocation in the House. If only Muslims were more clever politically, he told his New Jersey listeners, they could take over the United States and replace its constitutional government with a caliphate. "If we were united and strong, we'd elect our own emir [leader] and give allegiance to him. . . . [T]ake my word, if 6–8 million Muslims unite in America, the country will come to us." In 1995, Wahaj served as a character witness for Omar Abdel Rahman in the trial that found that blind sheikh guilty of conspiracy to overthrow the government of the United States. More alarming still, the U.S. attorney for New York listed Wahaj as one of the "unindicted persons who may be alleged as co-conspirators" in the sheikh's case.

The disparity between Wahaj's good citizenship in the House and his militant forecast of a Muslim takeover—not to mention his association with violent felons—is only one example of a larger pattern common to the American Muslim scene. Another example, about which I have written recently elsewhere, involves the American Muslims for Jerusalem, an organization whose official advocacy of "a Jerusalem that symbolizes religious tolerance and dialogue" contrasts markedly with the wild conspiracy-mongering and crude anti-Jewish rhetoric in which its spokesmen indulge at closed events, according to the *Jerusalem Post*. At a minimum, then, anyone who would understand the real views of American Muslims must delve deeper than the surface of their public statements.

Doing so, one discovers that the ambition to take over the United States is hardly a new one. The first missionaries for militant Islam, or Islamism, who arrived here from abroad in the 1920's, unblushingly declared, "Our plan is, we are going to conquer America." The audacity of such statements hardly went unnoticed at the time, including by Christians who cherished their own missionizing hopes. As a 1922 newspaper commentary put it:

> To the millions of American Christians who have so long looked eagerly forward to the time the cross shall be supreme in every land and the people of the whole world shall have become the followers of Christ, the plan to win this continent to the path of the "infidel Turk" will seem a thing unbelievable. But there is no doubt about its being pressed with all the fanatical zeal for which the Mohammedans are noted.

But it is in recent decades, as the Muslim population in the country has increased significantly in size, social standing, and influence, and as Islamism has made its presence widely felt on the international scene, that this "fanatical zeal" has truly come into its own. A catalyzing figure in the story is the late Ismail Al-Faruqi, a Palestinian immigrant who founded the International Institute of Islamic Thought and taught for many years at Temple University in Philadelphia. Rightly called "a pioneer in the development of Islamic studies in America," he was also the first contemporary theorist of a United States made Muslim. "Nothing could be greater," Al-Faruqi wrote in the early 1980's, "than this youthful, vigorous, and rich continent [of North America] turning away from its past evil and marching forward under the banner of Allahu Akbar [God is great]."

Al-Faruqi's hopes are today widely shared among educated Muslim leaders. Zaid Shakir, formerly the Muslim chaplain at Yale University, has stated that Muslims cannot accept the legitimacy of the American secular system, which "is against the orders and ordainments of Allah." To the contrary, "The orientation of the Qur'an pushes us in the exact opposite direction." To Ahmad Nawfal, a leader of the Jordanian Muslim Brethren who speaks frequently at American Muslim rallies, the United States has "no thought, no values, and no ideals"; if militant Muslims "stand up, with the ideology that we possess, it will be very easy for us to preside over this world." Masudul Alam Choudhury, a Canadian professor of business, writes matter-of-factly and enthusiastically about the "Islamization agenda in North America."

Islamism has made its presence widely felt on the international scene.

For a fuller exposition of this outlook, one can do no better than to turn to a 1989 book by Shamim A. Siddiqi, an influential commentator on American Muslim issues. Cryptically titled *Methodology of Dawah Ilallah in American Perspective* (more idiomatically rendered as "The Need to Convert Americans to Islam"), this 168-page study, published in Brooklyn, remains largely unavailable to general readers (neither amazon.com nor bookfinder.com listed it over a period of months) but is widely posted on Islamist websites, where it enjoys a faithful readership. In it, in prose that makes up in intensity and vividness for what it lacks in sophistication and polish, Siddiqi lays out both a detailed rationale and a concrete plan for Islamists to take over the United States and establish "Islamic rule" (iqamat ad-din).

Why America?

In Siddiqi's judgment, the need to assume control here is even more pressing than the need to sustain the revolution of the mullahs in Iran or to destroy Israel, for doing so will have a much greater positive impact on the future of Islam. America is central not for the reasons one might expect—its large population, its wealth, or the cultural influence it wields around the world—but on three other grounds.

The first has to do with Washington's role as the premier enemy of Islamism (or, possibly, of Islam itself). In Siddiqi's colorful language, whenever and wherever Muslims have moved toward establishing an Islamic state, the "treacherous hands of the secular West are always there . . . to bring about [their] defeat." Nor are Muslim rulers of any help, for they are "all in the pockets of the Western powers." If, therefore, Islam is ever going to attain its rightful place of dominance in the world, the "ideology of Islam [must] prevail over the mental horizon of the American people." The entire future of the Muslim world, Siddiqi concludes, "depends on how soon the Muslims of America are able to build up their own indigenous movement."

Secondly, America is central because establishing Islamism here would signal its final triumph over its only rival, that bundle of Christianity and liberalism which constitutes contemporary Western civilization. (One cannot help noting the irony that Siddiqi's tract appeared in the same year, 1989, as Francis Fukuyama's famous article speculating that, with the collapse of Communism and the apparent triumph of liberal democracy, we had begun to approach the "end of history.") And thirdly, and still more grandly, the infusion of the United States with Islamism would make for so powerful a combination of material success and spiritual truth that the establishment of "God's Kingdom" on earth would no longer be "a distant dream."

But this dream will not happen by itself. To American Muslims, writes Siddiqi, falls the paramount responsibility of bringing Islam to power in their country; and to this goal, Muslims must devote "all of their energies, talents, and resources." For this is how they will be assessed on judgment day: "Every Muslim living in the West will stand in the witness box in the mightiest court of Allah . . . in Akhirah [the last day] and give evidence that he fulfilled his responsibility, . . . that he left no stone unturned to bring the message of the Qur'an to every nook and corner of the country."

How this desired end is to be achieved is a question on which opinions differ in Siddiqi's world. Basically, the disagreement centers on the role of violence.

As has been made irrefutably clear, there are indeed some, not just abroad but living among us, who see the United States as (in the phrase of Osama bin Laden) an "enemy of Islam" that must be brought to its knees and destroyed. In its broad outlines, this judgment came to be solidified during the crisis over Iraq's seizure of Kuwait in the early 1990's, when militants like bin Laden discerned a historic parallel between the presence of American troops on the soil of Saudi Arabia and the brutal Soviet occupation of Afghanistan in the 1980's. In their dialectical view, as the *New Yorker* writer Mary Ann Weaver has explained, the United States, just like the Soviet Union before it, represented "an infidel occupation force propping up a corrupt, repressive, and un-Islamic government." And just as the Islamist mujahideen in Afghanistan had succeeded in defeating and driving out their occupiers, and thereby played a role in the collapse of the mighty Soviet Union itself, so Islamists might cause the collapse of the United States: one down, one to go, as it were.

To the blind sheikh Omar Abdel Rahman, who after bin Laden is perhaps today's most notorious enemy of the United States, bombing the World Trade Center in 1993 was part and parcel of this revolutionary strategy to "conquer the land of the infidels" by force. The idea, as one of his followers put it, was to "bring down their highest buildings and the mighty constructions they are so proud of, in order thoroughly to demoralize them," according to the writings of Egyptian immigrant Sayyid Abd al-Aziz Nusayr. And this was a duty that Islamists saw as incumbent on all Muslims; having helped humiliate the Soviets in Afghanistan, they now, as one native-born American convert to Islam proclaimed in July 1989, must "complete the march of jihad until we reach America and liberate her."

But there are several problems with the approach of revolutionary violence, even from the perspective of those who share its goal. The most obvious has to do with its impact on American society. Although attacks like the 1993 bombing or the suicide massacres of September 11, 2001, are intended to demoralize the American people, prompt civil unrest, and weaken the country politically, what they do instead is to bring Americans together in patriotism and purpose. Those who mastermind them, in the meantime, are often caught: Abdel Rahman is sitting out a life sentence in a federal penitentiary, his campaign of violence stillborn, while Osama bin Laden is the object of a massive manhunt to get him "dead or alive." Unlike in the very different case of the Soviet Union, it is hard to see how the use of force will succeed in wearing down this country, much less lead to a change in government.

Besides, as a number of commentators have recently pointed out, in targeting all Americans the perpetrators of Islamic violence do not bother even to discriminate between non-Muslim and Muslim victims. According to preliminary estimates, several hundred Muslims died in the collapse of the World Trade Center. This is not exactly calculated to enlist the participation of most resident Muslims in a campaign of violent insurrection.

Non-violent takeover

For all these reasons, the non-violent way would seem to have a brighter future, and it is in fact the approach adopted by most Islamists. Not only is it legal, but it allows its enthusiasts to adopt a seemingly benign view of the United States, a country they mean to rescue and make over rather than to destroy, and it dictates a strategy of working with Americans rather than against them. As a teacher at an Islamic school in Jersey City, near New York, explains, the "short-term goal is to introduce Islam. In the long term, we must save American society." Step by step, writes a Pakistan-born professor of economics, by offering "an alternative model" to Americans,

Muslims can refashion what Ismail Al-Faruqi called "the unfortunate realities of North America" into something acceptable in God's eyes.

Practically speaking, there are two main prongs to the non-violent strategy. The first involves radically increasing the number of American Muslims, a project that on the face of it would not seem very promising. Islam, after all, is still an exotic growth in the United States, its adherents representing just 1 to 2 percent of the population and with exceedingly dim prospects of becoming anything like a majority. Islamists are not so unrealistic as to think that these numbers can be substantially altered any time soon by large-scale immigration (which is politically unfeasible and might anyway provoke a backlash) or by normal rates of reproduction. Hence they focus most of their efforts on conversion.

> *Establishing Islamism [in America] would signal its final triumph over . . . Christianity and liberalism.*

They do so not only as a matter of expediency but on principle. For Islamists, converting Americans is the central purpose of Muslim existence in the United States, the only possible justification for Muslims to live in an infidel land. In the view of Shamim Siddiqi, there is no choice in the matter—American Muslims are "ordained by Allah" to help replace evil with good, and otherwise "have no right even to breathe." "Wherever you came from," adds Siraj Wahaj, "you came . . . for one reason—for one reason only—to establish Allah's din [faith]."

This imperative, relentlessly propagated by authoritative figures and promoted by leading Islamist organizations like the Muslim Student Association, has been widely adopted by Muslim Americans at large. Many attest to the sense of responsibility that flows from being an "ambassador for Islam," and are ever mindful of the cardinal importance of winning new adherents. And, given what they hold to be the truth of their message and the depravity of American culture, Islamists are optimistic about their chances of success. "A life of taqwah [piety] will immediately attract non-Muslims toward Islam," writes Abul Hasan Ali Nadwi, an important Indian Islamist, in his "Message for Muslims in the West."

He has a point: the more readily the message of Islam is available, the more converts it is likely to win. In making headway in the United States, Islam has largely depended on hands-on contact and personal experience. According to one survey, over two-thirds of American converts to Islam were motivated by the influence of a Muslim friend or acquaintance. *The Autobiography of Malcolm X* (1964), with its moving account of redemption through Islam, has had a wide impact on American blacks (and even some whites), causing a substantial number to convert. Similarly not to be discounted are the efforts of the various Muslim organizations in the United States, whose "attempts at educating the American public about Islam" may be responsible, according to one observer, for "Islam's increasing numbers."

But if increasing numbers are necessary, they are also not sufficient. After all, whole countries—Turkey, Egypt, Algeria—have overwhelmingly Muslim populations, but Islamism is suppressed by their governments.

From an Islamist point of view, indeed, the situation in Turkey is far worse than in the United States, for it is a more grievous thing to reject the divine message as interpreted by Islamists than merely to be ignorant of it. Therefore, in addition to building up Muslim numbers, Islamists must prepare the United States for their own brand of ideology. This means doing everything possible toward creating an Islamist environment and applying Islamic law. Activities under this heading fall into various categories.

Promoting Islamic rituals and customs in the public square. Islamists want secular authorities to permit students in public institutions, for example, to recite the basmallah (the formula "In the name of God, the Merciful, the Compassionate") in classroom exercises. They also want the right to broadcast over outdoor loudspeakers the five daily Islamic calls-to-prayer. Similarly, they have agitated for publicly maintained prayer facilities in such institutions as schools and airports.

Privileges for Islam. Islamists seek public financial support for Islamic schools, mosques, and other institutions. They also lobby for special quotas for Muslim immigrants, try to compel corporations to make special allowances for Muslim employees, and demand the formal inclusion of Muslims in affirmative-action plans.

Restricting or disallowing what others may do. Islamists want law-enforcement agencies to criminalize activities like drinking and gambling that are offensive to Islam. While seeking wide latitude for themselves, for instance when it comes to expressing disrespect for American national symbols, they would penalize expressions of disrespect for religious figures whom Islam deems holy, especially the prophet Muhammad; punish criticism of Islam, Islamism, or Islamists; and close down critical analysis of Islam.

The more readily the message of Islam is available, the more converts it is likely to win.

Some of these aims have already been achieved. Others may seem relatively minor in and of themselves, implying no drastic alterations in existing American arrangements but rather only slight adjustments in our already expansive accommodation of social "diversity." Cumulatively, however, by whittling away at the existing order, they would change the country's whole way of life—making Islam a major public presence, ensuring that both the workplace and the educational system accommodate its dictates and strictures, adapting family customs to its code of conduct, winning it a privileged position in American life, and finally imposing its system of law. Steps along the way would include more radical and intrusive actions like prohibiting conversion out of Islam, criminalizing adultery, banning the consumption of pork, formalizing enhanced rights for Muslims at the expense of non-Muslims, and doing away with equality of the sexes.

A Muslim majority? Islamic law the law of the land? Even the most optimistic Islamists concede the task will not be easy. Just as Muhammad confronted die-hard opponents in pagan Mecca, writes Siddiqi, so pious Muslims in America will face opponents, led by the "secular press cum media, the agents of capitalism, the champions of atheism (Godless creeds) and the [Christian] missionary zealots." Doing battle with them will demand focus, determination, and sacrifice.

And yet Siddiqi also thinks Muslims enjoy advantages undreamt of in Muhammad's day or in any other society than today's United States. For one thing, Americans are hungry for the Islamist message, which "pinpoints the shortcoming of capitalism, elaborates the fallacies of democracy, [and] exposes the devastating consequences of the liberal lifestyle." For another, the United States permits Islamists to pursue their political agenda in an entirely legal fashion and without ever challenging the existing order. Indeed, precisely because the Constitution guarantees freedom of religion, the system can be used to further Islamist aims. Democratic means are at hand for developing an active and persistent lobby, cultivating politicians, and electing Muslim representatives. Nearly a million legal immigrants arrive in the country each year, plus many more through the long coastlines and porous land borders. The courts are an all-important resource, and have already proved their worth in winning concession after concession from American corporations and public authorities.

Even so, the road will not be completely smooth. A delicate point will be reached, in Siddiqi's mind, as society polarizes between Muslim and non-Muslim camps "in every walk of life." At that point, as the struggle between Truth and Error "acquires momentum and the tension increases along with it," the "Wrong Doers" are likely to take desperate steps to "eliminate the Islamic movement and its workers by force." But if Islamists tread cautiously to navigate this point, taking special care not to alienate the non-Muslim population, eventually there will follow what Siddiqi calls a general "Rush-to-Islam." It will then be only a matter of time before Muslims find themselves not just enfranchised but actually running the show.

How much time? Siddiqi sees Islamists in power in Washington before 2020. For Wahaj, implementation of the shari'a in the United States "appears to be approaching fast," and in contemplating what that means his language grows ecstatic:

> I have a vision in America: Muslims owning property all over, Muslim businesses, factories, halal meat, supermarkets, all these buildings owned by Muslims. Can you see the vision, can you see the Newark International Airport and a John Kennedy Airport and LaGuardia having Muslim fleets of planes, Muslim pilots? Can you see our trucks rolling down the highways, Muslim names? Can you imagine walking down the streets of Teaneck [New Jersey]: three Muslim high schools, five Muslim junior-high schools, fifteen public schools? Can you see the vision, can you see young women walking down the street of Newark, New Jersey, with long flowing hijab and long dresses? Can you see the vision of an area of no crime, controlled by the Muslims?

A farfetched goal

It hardly needs pointing out that this vision is, to say the least, farfetched, or that Islamists are deluding themselves if they think that today's newborns will be attending college in an Iranian-style United States. But neither is their effort altogether quixotic: their devotion, energy, and skill are not to be questioned, and the larger Muslim-American community for which they claim to speak is assuredly in a position, especially as its numbers grow, to affect our public life in decisive ways. Indeed, despite persistent complaints of bias against them—more voluminous than ever in the wake of the airplane hijackings on September 11, 2001—Muslim Americans have built an enviable record of socioeconomic accomplishment in this country, have won wide public acceptance of their faith, and have managed to make it particularly difficult for anyone to criticize their religion or customs.

Whether and to what degree the community as a whole subscribes to the Islamist agenda are, of course, open questions. But what is not open to question is that, whatever the majority of Muslim Americans may believe, most of the organized Muslim community agrees with the Islamist goal—the goal, to say it once again, of building an Islamic state in America. To put it another way, the major Muslim organizations in this country are in the hands of extremists.

[Extremists are] hostile to the prevailing order in the United States.

One who is not among them is Muhammad Hisham Kabbani of the relatively small Islamic Supreme Council of America. In Kabbani's reliable estimation, such "extremists" have "taken over 80 percent of the mosques" in the United States. And not just the mosques: schools, youth groups, community centers, political organizations, professional associations, and commercial enterprises also tend to share a militant outlook, hostile to the prevailing order in the United States and advocating its replacement with an Islamic one.

Not all these organizations and spokesmen are open about their aspirations, though some are: for example, the International Institute of Islamic Thought in Herndon, Virginia, proclaims its academic purpose to be nothing less than "the Islamization of the humanities and the social sciences." But the best-known organizations—the ones whose members are invited to offer prayers and invocations before Congress or to attend White House functions, or whose representatives accompanied President George W. Bush on his September 17, 2001, visit to a mosque—tend to hide their true colors behind arch-respectable goals. Thus, the American Muslim Council claims to work "toward the political empowerment of Muslims in America," the Council on American-Islamic Relations is "putting faith into action," and the Muslim Public Affairs Council seeks only to make American Muslims "an influential component in U.S. public affairs."

But as I have documented at greater length on other occasions, much if not everything about the conduct of these organizations points to their essential agreement with the "conquer America" agenda, and from time to time their leaders—including Al-Faruqi and Shakir—have even said as much. As for Siraj Wahaj, he is a top figure in the Council on American-

Islamic Relations, the Islamic Society of North America, the Muslim Alliance in North America, and the Muslim Arab Youth Association, and his views contaminate every single one of them. It is not accurate to say, as President Bush said of the Islamist leaders with whom he met on September 17, 2001, that they "love America as much as I do."

That a significant movement in this country aspires to erode its bedrock social and legal arrangements, including the separation of church and state, and has even developed a roadmap toward that end, poses a unique dilemma, especially at this moment. Every responsible public official, and every American of good faith, is bent on drawing a broad distinction between terrorists operating in the name of Islam and ordinary Muslim "moms and dads." It is a true and valid distinction, but it goes much too far, and if adhered to as a guideline for policy it will cripple the effort that must be undertaken to preserve our institutions.

What such an effort would look like is a subject unto itself, but at a minimum it would have to entail the vigilant application of social and political pressure to ensure that Islam is not accorded special status of any kind in this country, the active recruitment of moderate Muslims in the fight against Islamic extremism, a keener monitoring of Muslim organizations with documented links to Islamist activity, including the support of terrorism, and the immediate reform of immigration procedures to prevent a further influx of visitors or residents with any hint of Islamist ideology. Wherever that seditious and totalitarian ideology has gained a foothold in the world, it has wrought havoc, and some societies it has brought to utter ruin. The preservation of our existing order can no longer be taken for granted; it needs to be fought for.

7

Islam Is Not a Threat to the West

Antony T. Sullivan

Antony T. Sullivan has written some eighty book chapters, journal articles, and academic reviews focusing on Arab and Islamic history and relations between the West and the Muslim world. He has lectured at some seventy universities and public policy institutes in the United States and overseas. He has served as an instructor in history at International College in Beirut, Lebanon, and as a lecturer in history at Hillsdale College, Michigan. Since 1988, Sullivan has held an appointment as associate for the Center for Middle Eastern and North African Studies at the University of Michigan.

The War on Terrorism, which was a response to the terrorist attacks on September 11, 2001, should be fought only against those involved in the attacks, not against Muslim civilizations. The terrorist attack was a violation of Islamic principles, such as mercy and compassion, that are advocated in the Koran, and the terrorists do not represent pious Muslims. Much of Islamic terrorists' antipathy toward Americans stems from specific American foreign policies, such as support for Israel, rather than from Islamic faith. The popular tendency to depict Islam as an enemy of the West will worsen already strained relations between the West and the Middle East.

I slam—as a religion, culture and society—most emphatically is not an enemy of the West.

Those who argue the contrary slander not only the third and last of the three great Abrahamic revelations but make all too likely the outbreak of either a religious war pitting Christianity (and perhaps Judaism) against Islam or a war of civilizations pitting the West against the entire Muslim world. And be assured: Any wars of religion or civilization will not be wars that the West—or the United States—will win.

This, of course, does not mean that the war [against terrorism] should not be prosecuted in the most energetic, merciless and sustained fashion possible. But to the extent feasible it should be fought as a guerre de l'ombre (a war in the shadows), focusing on destruction of the Afghani sources of international terrorism and the overthrow of the Taliban regime. Unless incontrovertible evidence is adduced of involvement of any state other than Afghanistan in the terrorist operation of September 11, 2001, public bombing or ground campaigns should be limited to Afghanistan alone. Under no circumstances should the war be permitted to degenerate into any "war of civilizations" or to be perceived by Arabs or Muslims as such.

Any wars of religion or civilization will not be wars that the West . . . will win.

Years before the attack on the World Trade Center and the Pentagon in September 2001, distinguished scholars such as professors Samuel Huntington of Harvard University and Bernard Lewis of Princeton University, and publicists such as Daniel Pipes and Steven Emerson, were suggesting the possibility of clashes between Islam and the West, and the likelihood that Muslims worldwide might support terrorism to destroy Western civilization. Their work, implicitly or explicitly, prepared the ground for the U.S. Anti-Terrorism Act of 1996 and the consequent jailings without charge of up to 19 Arabs or Muslims in the United States. At least one of the individuals imprisoned was held for more than three years. No evidence of culpability of any of these individuals ever was adduced publicly, and most of these Arab or Muslim detainees are fortunately now free on court order. Ideas—particularly those of distinguished scholars—do have consequences, and bad ideas may indeed have very bad consequences.

The three Abrahamic faiths

Judaism, Christianity and Islam all trace their origins back at least to the Old Testament prophet Abraham. Each of these three religions venerates him. Each of these Abrahamic faiths has similarities with the other two, and each historically has produced civilizations and societies with recognizably similar characteristics.

Not only is Islam not an enemy of the West, but it, like Judaism, is part of the larger civilizational ecumene that we in the contemporary West know—or ought to. In fact, the West stops at the Indus, not at the Dardanelles. Today, Islam is part and parcel of the West, just as the West is part and parcel of Islam.

What occurred on September 11, 2001, was first and foremost an attack on Islam itself. Specifically, that criminal operation constituted an attack on the values of compassion, beneficence and mercy that pervade the Koran and that historically have characterized the practice of Islam. The ignorant terrorists responsible for the operation of September 11, 2001, might have done well to reread the fatiha (the eight opening lines) of the Koran. There, they would have found compassion and mercy mentioned a total of four times.

And they would have done well to read Chapter 5, Verse 32 of the Koran: "We prescribed . . . that whosoever kills a person, unless it be for manslaughter or for mischief in the land, it is as though he had killed all mankind. And whosoever saves a life, it is as though he had saved the lives of all men."

Moreover, had they consulted additional portions of the Koran, they might have discovered that the planned operation only could have been undertaken by Muslim apostates. To the extent that the Koran endorses war at all, it endorses only defensive combat designed to protect the Islamic community in the most dire of circumstances. No faithful Muslim possibly could justify the operation of September 11, 2001, within that limitation.

The Koran includes passages invoking violence. But so does the Old Testament, in considerable number. To wit, Deuteronomy 32:42: "I will make my arrows drank with blood, and my sword shall devour flesh; and that with the blood of the slain and of the captives, from the long-haired heads of the enemy" (see also Deuteronomy 2:34, 3:6 and 7:2). Evocations of violence in religious texts is one of many elements the Abrahamic religions share.

Contemporary terrorists who invoke Islam to justify their actions are utterly ignorant of classical Islamic law. Muslim jurisprudence is categorical: It prescribes the harshest penalties, including death, for terrorism. Crimes defined as terroristic and/or criminal in classical jurisprudence include the poisoning of wells, abduction, brigandage, night assaults and rape. Modern terrorists who proclaim themselves Muslims seem unaware that the Koran makes clear that the injustice of others in no way excuses any injustice of one's own.

For almost a decade Muslim religious leaders and public figures have been sponsoring international conferences designed to demonstrate the fallacy of any notion of Islam being an enemy of the West or the likelihood of any clash of civilizations. I know, because I have participated in several of these conferences. Those who persist in merchandising notions of Islam being an enemy of the West should know that there is an almost universal rejection of this idea in the Muslim world itself. Such writers mislead Western public opinion and alienate Muslims everywhere who otherwise might be only too glad to be friends with the West.

Islam is part and parcel of the West, just as the West is part and parcel of Islam.

The September 11, 2001, attack has been publicly and categorically condemned by the most important Islamist leaders and public figures in the world. On September 24, 2001, the London-based Arabic daily *al Quds al Arabi* published a statement in which more than 75 such individuals forcefully denounced the "terrorist aggression on large American installations which killed innocent victims belonging to more than 60 countries." They described the tragedy as a "crime against humanity" and called upon all believers in the sanctity of human life to "denounce and fight against terrorism wherever it is and regardless of the ethnicity or religion of those involved in it." These Islamists added that "all those proved to have committed terrorist acts against humanity . . . should be tried and punished, without any kind of allowances."

Rather than any antipathy emanating from Islam, Americans and other Westerners should recognize that anger toward the United States in the Muslim world emanates primarily from the rage at specific American policies. U.S. partiality to Israel at the expense of Palestinians, maintenance of sanctions on Iraq that fail to weaken Saddam Hussein while resulting in the death of half-a-million Iraqi children, and consistent failure to support individual liberty and limited government in Muslim states are among their major grievances. Those who pontificate on Islam somehow being an enemy of the West almost never mention or grant any legitimacy to this list of complaints. And these grievances are fully shared by the 7 million American citizens who now are Muslim.

One of the most promising contemporary initiatives in interfaith and intercivilizational dialogue is the Circle of Tradition and Progress, which brings together distinguished Western and Muslim (Islamist) thinkers to explore and combat the worldwide challenge of radical modernity. The philosophic basis for this joint enterprise is the thought (from the Western tradition) of such thinkers as Thomas Aquinas, Edmund Burke, Eric Voegelin, Gerhart Niemeyer and Russell Kirk. Muslim participants adduce Islamic thinkers of similar philosophic orientations. In distinction to speculations about impending civilizational conflict, the Circle of Tradition and Progress represents a practical ecumenical endeavor whereby the West and the Islamic world may jointly address the viruses of modernity that today so threaten us all.

The statement of purpose of the Circle of Tradition and Progress offers sage advice on how to conduct international relations. The statement reads: "We favor the conduct of international relations on a basis of respect for all the world's civilizations. We oppose all attempts to export or impose cultural systems, to support dictatorial regimes or to obstruct democratic transformation. It is our conviction that attempts to reinvent the Cold War with Muslims targeted as enemies of the West, or the West as enemies of Islam, are deplorable and should be avoided. We are united in our belief that all such Manichaean formulations will impede cooperation between Muslims and the West, and are likely over time to have a dramatically negative impact on both international stability and world peace." Bush-administration officials charged with responding to the September 11, 2001, attack might well be guided by such counsel.

Popular perception

If the contemporary tendency to depict Islam as an enemy of the West is unconscionable, it also is understandable. So is the popular receptivity to this perverse idea that characterizes Western culture.

The roots of this disposition reach back at least as far as the Crusades. The Western conviction of an alien and menacing Islamic "other" was solidified by the centuries of war between the Ottoman Empire and Western and Central Europe. It was exacerbated by European colonialism and the Christian missionary enterprise of the 19th century and the evangelical revival today, and it currently flourishes as a result of the serious challenge that the Islamic revival presents to the long-term viability of the state of Israel.

It is not by chance that those most frequently proclaiming that Islam is an enemy of the West are themselves fervent partisans of Israel or (as in the case of former Israeli prime minister Benjamin Netanyahu), Israelis themselves. Islam is in no way a challenge to the West, but in its political form it may well present a threat to Israel. If so, that is Israel's problem, not ours. Israel alone can mitigate any Islamic threat only by dealing justly with all its neighbors, and most specifically with the Palestinians.

As a Republican and a conservative, I call on my philosophical comrades in arms to reject the anti-Islamic triumphalist warmongering of neoconservative ideologues. And I urge all Americans to repudiate any belief that Islam is an enemy of the West. This idea is wrong. Worse, it is dangerous. To all of us. Especially now.

Islamic Fundamentalist Schools Foster Terrorism

Tashbih Sayyed

Tashbih Sayyed is editor-in-chief of In Review, *a quarterly journal of the United States Institute of Strategic Studies for South Asia, and of* Pakistan Today, *a weekly national newspaper published in California.*

Wahabiism, a rigid, fundamentalist division of Islam, has been steadily growing since the 1970s. Wahabis established schools in Muslim countries, known as *madrasas*, in which they teach children that Jews and Americans are responsible for the rampant poverty and political turmoil in the Middle East. These teachings instill such resentment against the West that former *madrasa* students often commit acts of terrorism, such as the September 11, 2001, attack on America. America's war against terrorism must involve reversing a culture of hatred and teaching children in Middle Eastern countries the values of democracy and freedom. America should provide financial aid to destitute countries and ensure that the money is used to instill in children positive, democratic values.

This first war of the new millennium is a war of minds. This war will not be won by conquering bodies and real estate, but rather minds and hearts. This war is to be waged on a different kind of battlefield—in the religious academies and schools. The weapons in this war will have to be different. They will have to change the circumstances that give birth to such a state of mind. We will have to remember that poverty, ignorance and absence of basic human rights give birth to anger and frustration. Extremists can harness these feelings to further their destructive goals.

Those who attacked the World Trade Center and the Pentagon on September 11, 2001, are products of a culture of hatred. This culture evolved over the course of decades and grew out of several sources. To overcome it, Western policymakers should take notice of its origins and vital elements.

The most important of these has been the development of Wahabiism in Saudi Arabia, which preaches a very narrow and rigid interpretation of Islam based on its hatred of Zionism and the United States. It preaches that all the miseries that Muslims suffer are caused by a Judeo-Christian conspiracy backed by the United States. In the view of Wahabiism, a global theocratic "Islam" will follow the destruction of the United States and Israel. Until Saudi Arabia got its windfall of petro dollars in the 1970s, Wahabiism was slow in recruiting its cadre. Its exponents told the Muslims that Jews, with the help of the United States, kept Muslims in economic, social and cultural bondage. They blamed Zionism for destruction of the Ottoman Empire, the establishment of the state of Israel and the total humiliation of Muslims around the world. Wahabiism promises to avenge the centuries-old insults and degradation that Muslims have suffered at the hands of Western industrialized countries as well as Zionism.

Teaching vengeance

Adherents established academies known as madrasas to indoctrinate young Muslim minds in this theory. Saudi petro dollars provided the movement with funds to establish madrasas in Pakistan, India and Bangladesh. In my experience these madrasas have only one objective: to breed Islamic jihadists committed to either convert or eliminate all non-Wahabis everywhere.

Because of the socioeconomic conditions prevailing in Pakistan and Afghanistan, the madrasas have had no problem finding students. By the time the Soviets invaded Afghanistan, madrasas had enough numbers to put up an impressive resistance against them. Even U.S. officials were impressed when they encountered in the jihad movement a potent Cold War ally. What U.S. handlers did not know then was that, to these jihadists, there was no difference between Moscow and Washington—both were infidels. They were fighting their war, not that of the United States.

During the Soviet occupation of Afghanistan the United States dumped billions of dollars into the hands of Pakistan's military dictator, General Mohammad Zia ul-Haq, a devout Wahabi himself. He steered some of these funds toward establishing a network of madrasas to train and educate future recruits for the mujahideen. He urged the extremist Wahabi Muslims to establish as many madrasas as they could and to do this as quickly as possible.

> *Those who attacked the World Trade Center and the Pentagon on September 11, 2001, are products of a culture of hatred.*

Poverty, ignorance, hunger and the absence of basic civil amenities were silent partners in recruitment with the fundamentalist clerics. Madrasas instructors conveniently attributed all these ills to the workings of a universal Judeo-Christian conspiracy to keep the Muslims backward. And the United States was cast as the leader of this conspiracy.

The war filled the madrasas with new students. In Afghanistan there is only one breadwinner in most families. Thousands of these breadwinners died in the war against the Soviets, leaving behind many thousands of widows and orphans. There was no social-security system to take care of them. Madrasas took advantage of the situation and offered to take these orphans off their mothers' hands. Afghan mothers were only too happy to find that the madrasas would take, feed, clothe, shelter and educate their children.

The curriculum was simple: memorization of the Koran, education in the most primitive ways of a very rigid Wahabiism and strenuous military training to fight the infidels. Children in these schools were forbidden to see anyone outside the madrasas and were not allowed to watch TV or listen to radio. They were virtually in a bubble totally insulated from the outside world. Day in and day out they were brainwashed into hating the infidels, especially the United States and Zionism.

Uprooting a culture of hatred

This culture does not owe its existence to any one particular leader but evolved as part of a popular psychology. Virtually all graduates of this culture are ready to die in the process of establishing their "Islamic" state. Needless to say, one may not get rid of the culture by eliminating its leaders. The whole environment has to be changed to eradicate this culture of terrorism.

[Islamism] has exported its revolution to all parts of the world.

It took almost 40 years for this culture to grow into a formidable "ism"—Islamism. In this period few realized that Islamism was more dangerous than communism. It has not only conquered Afghanistan but also besieged Pakistan from within. It has exported its revolution to all parts of the world. September 11, 2001, proved that even the United States is not beyond its reach.

Uprooting a culture of hatred will mean educating masses of children in Afghanistan, Pakistan and other countries. At the same time, education only can be provided in a society that enjoys basic amenities of life—food, clothing, shelter, health care. The provision of these basic amenities in turn needs an economic structure that provides employment to a majority of the people.

Such an effort requires a strategy along the lines of the Marshall Plan provided by the United States to [offer economic aid to] Europe in the aftermath of World War II. To accomplish this goal the United States will have to stay on in Afghanistan after having achieved its immediate goals of defeating the Taliban and capturing terrorist Osama bin Laden in order to oversee the establishment of an environment that does not breed hatred. The United States has to help in building socioeconomic resources that provide a bare minimum of civic amenities to the masses so that the reason for their anger is eliminated.

The plan's objective has to be creation of a future generation that believes in the values of democracy, freedom and liberty. Satisfied and content people can afford to send their children to real schools instead of madrasas.

To achieve this objective a strict watch must be maintained on what is being taught in the educational institutions in these countries. Islamists took 40 years to overwhelm the world with graduates of their madrasas. We will have to be equally patient. While working to counter the extremist mind, we will have to make sure that the affected societies start reaping the benefits of the new Marshall Plan so that there is a support system available for these new minds to prosper.

Aiding specific programs

Countries receiving aid under this new plan must not be allowed to spend it on defense or pet projects of regime cronies. All programs established under this plan will have the aim of uplifting the standard of living of the masses. Program administrators must show that standards of education and health steadily are on the rise as aid investments flow into the country. Labor-intensive industries should be encouraged so that the maximum number of people can find employment.

True, to ensure that such a plan succeeds, aid-granting nations must keep a strict watch over the benefitting governments. In the past, much of the aid the United States gave for the economic development of countries was misappropriated by rulers such as Joseph Mobuto in Zaire, Ferdinand Marcos in the Philippines, Zia in Pakistan, Saddam Hussein in Iraq, etc., leaving the masses poorer than before. The corruption of these dictators and kings has made the United States a villain in the eyes of the poorest citizens.

However, aid can be dispensed incrementally and with careful verification of distribution, as the World Bank has learned to do in recent years. For a large-scale assistance plan such as this to succeed, its paramount objective must be to ensure that the values of democracy, freedom and liberty become the focus of the new curriculum being taught in the schools.

It is a hopeful sign that Secretary of State Colin Powell, in meetings with Pakistan's military ruler General Pervez Musharraf, reportedly called on Pakistan to do something about the system of fundamentalist religious schools that serve as breeding grounds for militant anti-Americanism and support for the Taliban.

To reform madrasas, two steps must be taken. First, the state has to approve the curriculum. Second, a modern and scientific teacher-training program must be introduced to ensure that no person with extremist and fundamentalist views gets a teaching license.

Would extremist and fundamentalist Muslims accept the new and reformed madrasas? They would if the state protects moderate clerics ready and willing to issue edicts condemning extremism, which really is the requirement in Islam. Fundamentalists have great respect for religious fatwas, and the state will have to encourage them. Islam is a faith of the middle path and rejects extremism in all its forms.

Islamist Terrorism Does Not Reflect Islam

Margot Patterson

Margot Patterson is a senior writer for the National Catholic Reporter, *a weekly, independent, Catholic journal.*

The terrorist attacks on September 11, 2001, have given rise to questions about whether the nature of Islam breeds terrorism or if rogue Muslims misinterpret the Koran. Some people argue that poverty and the lack of democracy in Muslim nations—not Islam—contributes to acts of terrorism. In fact, many contend that the Koran advocates tolerance and peace. Terrorists who claim to act in accordance with Islam manipulate the Koran's message to achieve domination and power.

President George W. Bush has insisted that the terrorist attacks of September 11, 2001, [when Islamic terrorists hijacked U.S. planes and crashed them into the World Trade Center and the Pentagon] and the U.S. response to them are not about Islam but about terrorism. In the immediate aftermath of the events, many agreed. Muslim clerics around the world denounced the terrorist attacks on New York and Washington that left approximately three thousand people dead.

While Osama bin Laden, the alleged instigator of the terrorist hijackings, portrayed the attacks and the retaliatory bombing by the United States as a clash of civilizations and called on Muslims to rise up against the infidels, a chorus of voices both inside and outside the Muslim world said bin Laden's views represented a perversion of Islam.

More recently, some voices have spoken out to suggest that the conflict between the United States and Osama bin Laden and his followers is more rooted in the nature of Islam than its defenders conveyed.

Writing for *The New York Times Magazine* in a piece titled "This is a Religious War," Andrew Sullivan argued that the religious dimensions of the conflict are central to its meaning.

Salman Rushdie wrote a November 2, 2001, *New York Times* opinion piece, "Yes, This is About Islam," in which he spoke of the need for a depoliticized Islam that would assume the secularist-humanist principles on which modernity is based. Novelist and Nobel prize–winner V.S. Naipaul, long a critic of Islam, assailed the religion once again in an interview published in the October 28, 2001, issue of *The New York Times Magazine*, asserting that a non-fundamentalist Islam was a contradiction in terms. More recently, *New York Times* columnist Thomas L. Friedman weighed in, arguing, "This is not about terrorism. Terrorism is just a tool. We're fighting to defeat an ideology: religious totalitarianism."

Suddenly Islam itself, not just Osama bin Laden and his terrorist network, is under scrutiny, the object of an intellectual inquisition about its values, its history and its compatibility with modern society.

Are the claims true? Is there something inherently intolerant in the nature of Islam that makes it maladapted to modernity and vulnerable to extremism?

In many cases the criticisms of Islam contain simplifications and misunderstandings.

These are tricky issues, both because of the complexity of Islam and the diverse range of beliefs within it, and because Osama bin Laden's brand of Islamic fundamentalism is entwined with political grievances that are widely shared by people in the Mideast, regardless of their religious beliefs.

Moreover, in many cases the criticisms of Islam contain simplifications and misunderstandings, not only about Islam but about Western culture and history.

"The key question always has to be, whose Islam are we talking about?" said Professor R.K. Ramazani, professor emeritus of government and foreign relations at the University of Virginia. "The reason for that is there are 1 billion Muslims in the world scattered all over the world from Indonesia to West Africa and they have extremely diverse subcultures. The way of looking at Islam in Egypt is not the same as in Saudi Arabia or in Iran. This is why it is so difficult to talk about whether Islam is prone to violence or fertile soil for terrorists."

It may be, in fact, the very diversity of Islam that accounts for the contradictions in speaking about it. Fawaz Gerges, a professor of international relations and Middle Eastern studies at Sarah Lawrence College, speaks of an authoritarian streak that runs through Muslim culture "from the dining table to the bedroom." On the other hand, he acknowledges that numerous factors other than religion are responsible for the lack of democratic institutions in the societies of the Middle East.

Few democrats

"How can you have democratic institutions if you have few democrats?" Gerges asked. "This has to do not just with Islam but with political culture, with socialization, with lack of economic growth, with hundreds of years of political oppression. Islam is just one factor in the equation.

"If you look at the various voices within Islam, they are highly diverse. You have enlightened voices, conservative voices, fascist and reactionary voices," said Gerges.

John O. Voll, professor of Islamic history at Georgetown University's Center for Christian-Muslim Understanding, notes that of the four most populous Muslim societies, two—Indonesia and Bangladesh—are competitive democracies with female heads of state. Of the other two, India is the world's largest democracy with a large Muslim minority that has actively participated in the political process since India was founded while Pakistan is currently a military dictatorship but also has some tradition of democracy.

Like Indonesia and Bangladesh, India and Pakistan have been headed by women, which should perhaps jostle some stereotypes of Islam, Voll said.

The Georgetown professor described Islam as no more ill prepared to cope with modernity or democracy than Christianity or Judaism.

"All you have to do is walk through the Mea Shearim area in Jerusalem and see the Hasidic Jews concentrated there, who have some difficulty accepting modernity. Or listen to Christian fundamentalists," he said. "Jerry Falwell has as much difficulty conceptually coping with global pluralism as bin Laden."

Similarly, the militancy some people ascribe to Islam is equally present in the other monotheistic religious traditions, where an emphasis on the primacy of one god and one truth leads to distinctions between believers and unbelievers. Intrinsic in Judaism, Christianity and Islam is the idea that you serve your God through charity and love and also through war, Voll said, noting that all three religions contain strains that make it possible to argue both for and against the concept of the just war.

People sometimes conveniently forget that while Jesus said, "Love your enemy," Jesus also said, "Do not think that I came to bring peace. I came to bring the sword," Voll said.

"In the same way, the Quran says fight against the unbeliever, and the Quran also says God created us as diverse people so we could learn from each other and compete with each other in doing good."

Some scholars suggest that the focus on Islam after the terrorist attacks is misleading because it bypasses anti-Americanism as a staple of Arab politics, irrespective of religion.

"The United States has managed to alienate most of the rising social classes in the Arab and Muslim world," said Gerges, author of *American and Political Islam: Clash of Interests or Clash of Cultures?* "The Islamists do not differ from other social and political groups in anti-American sentiment."

Accumulated grievances

Mumtaz Ahmad, professor of political science at Hampton University, Hampton, Va., noted that a host of grievances have accumulated in the Middle East. They relate both to America's perceived blind support for Israel, despite Israel's violations of U.N. resolutions and international laws, and to U.S. support for dictatorial, oppressive regimes that serve the United States' own short-term strategic purposes.

With no way of legally changing the regimes they live under, people are driven to violent, underground activities. Often the mosque is the only place where people can freely meet and mingle.

"Islam has become an important variable in this whole drama only because the people who indulge in terrorism are doing it in the name of Islam," Ahmad said. "That's the only Islamic relevance to the events of September 11, 2001. No less. No more."

Like others, Ahmad said Osama bin Laden's extremist viewpoints are unrepresentative of Islam. Ramazani calls bin Laden's views downright "un-Islamic" and a "fringe perspective within Islam."

The militancy some people ascribe to Islam is equally present in the other monotheistic religious traditions.

Fringe perspective it may be, but theologian Father James Fredericks believes it's a mistake to dismiss the religious faith bin Laden and his followers subscribe to as un-Islamic, even if it is atypical. Fredericks, a professor who teaches comparative theology at Loyola Marymount University in Los Angeles, draws an analogy with Christianity and its troubled and troubling history of anti-Semitism.

"The idea of justifying Christian anti-Semitism from the teaching of Jesus is just wrong," Fredericks said. "Therefore, there's the temptation to say that Christians who are anti-Semites are not true Christians. That kind of approach can excuse Christians from looking into their own tradition, and into some dark and ugly corners of the history of Christianity."

Muslims, too, have an obligation to look at their own tradition and the social, institutional, political and theological problems Islam faces, said Fredericks, who described Islam today as challenged both by secularism and the effects of colonialism.

"In United States we've worked out this tentative arrangement where religion is relegated to the private sphere but on occasion takes on this very public voice, like Martin Luther King," said Fredericks. "That is what Islam is struggling with. In a lot of Muslim societies, they've tried to become modern nations like in the West where religion is a purely private matter. What it's brought them is corruption, economic injustice, immorality and social inequality. So what I hear them saying is that no, this is not what we want. We don't want to become decadent like in the West. What we want is a society based on justice and morality, and we're not going to find this in the Western secular model."

Instead, many Muslims are looking to a revived and renewed Islam that will provide the basis for a just society. "Some of these Islamic voices are not all that different from Christian liberation theologians," Fredericks said. "Both are very public religious voices calling for justice and critiquing economic inequality and immorality."

Fredericks noted that Christianity's adaptation to pluralism and secularism is the result of long and painful struggle. It was only in 1965, at the Second Vatican Council, that the Roman Catholic church officially endorsed freedom of religion.

Today, he said, two kinds of Christians disagree with the current Western model of privatized religion: Jerry Falwell and Jesuit Father

Daniel Berrigan, both of whom believe Christian truth and morality should be very much in the public sphere.

Unlike Islam, Christianity worked out its way of living with modernity without also having to deal with the cultural interruption imposed by colonialism, Fredericks said.

"Modernity was forced on Islam through colonialism. The fact that we would have violent reactions and that we would have many, many voices in the Islamic world saying at times contradictory things should come as no surprise," said Fredericks.

"What Westerners need to take seriously is that the secular model is not the only option for being a modern nation. I don't think Westerners understand that. We just presume that any Muslims who say 'We want a Muslim society' are leading their people back to the 'Middle Ages.' Westerners can't imagine any other form of modernity than to be secular."

Graham Fuller, a former U.S. Foreign Service officer and a retired vice-chairman of the National Intelligence Council at the CIA, views the discussion of Islam as part of a broader discussion of the borderline between religion and politics that relates to all religions. Interestingly, in the case of Islam there are many more explicit ideals of good governance expressed in the Quran than there are in either the Hebrew Bible or the New Testament, Fuller said.

"The word democracy does not appear in the Bible, the Old and New Testament, but in the Quran and the words of the Prophet there is explicit recognition that one of the qualities of good governance is that the ruler must consult the people as to what is to be done. Muslim activists interpret that as meaning democratic government. Most Islamists strongly seek democracy in their own countries because they believe they would do well in such a system," he said. "They claim the United States does not want to see democracy come to the Middle East because the United States does not want Islamists to come to power, whether moderate or radical."

"What Westerners need to take seriously is that the secular model is not the only option for being a modern nation."

Like other commentators, Fuller said political Islam is simply one of the more potent contemporary expressions of a deep body of grievances that has developed in parts of the Muslim world. While many Muslim movements are turning to the political ideas expressed in the Quran as an inspiration for overturning unjust and corrupt regimes, only a tiny portion of those movements have turned violent, he said.

"To say the problem is in Islam any more than to say the basic problem in Northern Ireland is Christianity or acts of Jewish terror in Israel is Judaism . . . is to blame the religion for distortions or selective and narrow interpretations of it," said Fuller. Though Americans are focused on the dangers of religious extremism, Fuller said most Muslims would point out that the most hideous crimes of the 20th century were committed in Europe, not in the name of religion but ideology.

Americans focus on menace

If a common impression is that Islam is a religion of extremists, some scholars said it's in part because Americans, not unnaturally, are engaged by what they perceive as menacing.

"One of the reasons that Americans perceive Islam as anti-democratic and anti-pluralistic and prone to violence is that we tend to be more interested and engaged with those dimensions of Islam that are threatening to us and less interested in those dimensions that are compatible with our values," said R. Scott Appleby, a professor of history at the University of Notre Dame and the author of *The Ambivalence of the Sacred: Religion, Violence and Reconciliation.* "That image of Islam as a defiant force against the West, as a militant body seeking to overthrow democratic values, is precisely what the Islamic extremists want us to believe," Appleby said. "It's only a small part of the larger, more complex picture of Islam."

Some of the recent criticisms of Islam suggest that many American Christians misunderstand their own history.

One of the most common statements made about Islam today is that it needs a Reformation. That opinion, Voll noted, ignores the fact that the Reformation ushered in almost a century of Europe's bloodiest wars.

"People pick a symbol and then they conveniently forget the historical reality," Voll said. "What most people mean when they say what Islam needs is a Reformation is that it needs to have thinkers who reformulate Islamic theology in modern terms."

According to Voll, Islam has such thinkers. "The classic case is the great Egyptian intellectual Muhammad Abduh, who lived at the end of the 19th century and who provided a rearticulation of Islam in modern terms," Voll said.

The recent scrutiny of Islam may offer a mirror in which Americans can see not only others' values but their own. At least some of the responses to reports of Islamic terrorists' religious motivations suggest how far materially secure Americans have progressed toward secularism, how far removed is the power of religion as a motivating force.

In an essay titled "Visions of Sacrifice" in the October 17, 2001, issue of *The Christian Century*, Appleby discusses Attorney General John Ashcroft and journalist Bob Woodward's professions of shock at a letter written by Mohamed Atta, one of the September 11, 2001, hijackers, containing prayers and exhortations to martyrdom.

"One of the reasons America misunderstands Islam is that we've lost touch with the kind of devotion and self-sacrifice that traditional religion can evoke in its followers," Appleby told the *National Catholic Reporter.*

In his essay Appleby writes that Muslim extremists hate Americans because we cast off orthodox Christianity in the 1960s for a materialistic, liberalized, compromising approach to faith, which they despise in their own co-religionists.

"They hate us, most of all, for ignoring them and for underestimating the power of their faith," Appleby writes. "And faith it is, however twisted, distorted, un-Islamic and sinful we deem its expression."

10
Fundamentalism Exists Across All Religions

America

America is a weekly magazine that was founded by Jesuits in 1909.

Fundamentalism is not a uniquely Islamic phenomenon. All religions have evinced some form of fundamentalism, as evidenced by the Christian Crusades in the Middle Ages to modern atrocities against Muslims committed by Jews in Israel. Fundamentalism in any religion is a natural response to modernity. Moreover, other religions have only recently ended their violent and puritanical reactions to a changing world. Hopefully, the positive transformation of other religions will influence Muslims to accept the value of religious freedom and individuality.

We sometimes imagine that the besieged and occasionally violent form of religiosity known as fundamentalism is a uniquely Islamic trait. This is not the case. As novelist and former nun Karen Armstrong has written, "fundamentalism is a global fact and has surfaced in every major faith in response to the problems of modernity." American Christian fundamentalism began around 1900, and the Muslim variety surfaced in the 1950's. Islamic fundamentalists sought to move religion from the sidelines back to the center of life by withdrawing into an enclave of pure faith—as ultra-Orthodox Jewish communities do in Jerusalem and New York.

When Pope John Paul II and Mohammad Khatami, the president of Iran, met in Rome on March 11, 1999, there was much on which they agreed: the struggle against jahiliyyah—the "ignorance" or "barbarism" of the modern world. But for many Muslims the Koran allows no dichotomy between sacred and profane, religious and political; the aim is to integrate the whole of life in a community faithful to God. And fundamentalist Muslims invoke a strict and somewhat joyless reading of the law (shariah) over against the toleration and reconciliation the Prophet Muhammad preferred.

Violence and fundamentalism are not intrinsically linked, but violence has broken out in all forms of fundamentalism—in Christianity, Ju-

From "Islam and Modernity," *America*, November 12, 2001. Copyright © 2001 by America Press, Inc. Reprinted with permission.

daism, Islam, Hinduism, Sikhism and Confucianism. Remember the Branch Davidians in Texas [who held a violent fifty-one-day standoff with police in 1993]; Aum Shinrikyo, which gassed people in Tokyo subways; Baruch Goldstein, who machine-gunned scores of unarmed Muslim worshippers in Hebron in Israel; and, of course, Osama bin Laden.

All Islamic fundamentalists try to change the world. An early Pakistani fundamentalist, Abul Ala Mawdudi (1903–79), was one of the first to unite Muslims against the colonial West. Because God is alone sovereign, nobody is obliged to take orders from any other human. Revolution against the colonial powers is a duty, a universal jihad, Mawdudi argued.

Mawdudi influenced the Egyptian Sayyid Qutb (1906–66), who considered Gamal Abdel Nasser an enemy of the faith, an apostate, whose government Muslims were duty-bound to overthrow. After the defeat of Arab armies in the Six-Day War against Israel in 1967, Nasser lost credibility and the whole Middle East swung toward religion. Students and workers created mosques in universities and factories, where groups like the Muslim Brotherhood could set up welfare societies (health care, education, counseling, temporary housing) to demonstrate that Islam worked better than the government. Where modern culture had an alien tenor, fundamentalists provided meaning and a spirituality that was accessible to the people.

For the first time fundamentalism summoned young people from spectator status to an active participation in their culture and, more to the point, gave them a sense of meaning and purpose, something none of their leaders tried to do. The Iranian revolution of 1978–79 can be seen in this light. In the 1960's, Ayatollah Ruhollah Khomeini brought Iranians into the streets to die by the thousands to protest the policies of Muhammad Reza Shah.

Insidious fundamentalists

Many see Islam being taken over by a poisonous element, by small-minded theocrats who advocate cruel attitudes toward women, education, the economy and modern life in general. And one finds this all over, in Pakistan, India, Malaysia, Philippines and Indonesia—where the faith is policed by religious commissars. The West is hated because its pop culture is corrupting their youth with its music, films, consumer products and secular values. The globalized economy is seen as making the West richer and them poorer. And the West's support for Israel and its economic sanctions against Iraq are seen as attacks on Muslims.

Christianity's record of crusades, inquisitions and pogroms shows that it has been as puritanical and violent as anything we find now among rigid Islamic fundamentalists. Only recently did Catholics learn the value of separating church and state and of respecting religious freedom. American and European Muslims may be key actors in helping Islam learn the same lesson, just as American Catholics helped teach this lesson to Catholicism. Only a free commitment can be trusted. Muslims must learn how to renounce the use of state coercion to enforce their religious orthodoxies. Indeed, in rejecting proselytism or forced conversion, Muhammad recognized that only a free religion would guarantee both civic peace and a vibrant religious faith.

11

Islamic Fundamentalism Is Being Shaped by the West

John O'Sullivan

John O'Sullivan is an editor at the National Review. *His articles for the weekly magazine include "Sizing Up the Saudis," "Allegiances in a Multicultural Age," "Osama Outdated," and "Huddling with Terrorists."*

The terrorists that orchestrated the attacks on America on September 11, 2001, had been educated in the West and exposed to American culture and privilege. Their experiences in the West served to highlight the contrast between America's prosperity and the Middle East's poverty and political strife. Western success angered the Muslims, who considered themselves God's chosen people. While some Muslims embrace Western ways, others—such as those who committed the attacks on America—condemn and challenge them.

The more we learn about the men who destroyed the World Trade Center on September 11, 2001, the more mysterious they seem. That mystery does not, however, reside in their foreignness. Osama bin Laden, Mullah Omar, and various Muslim clerics with walk-on parts, hectoring crowds in Pakistan, look exotic enough in their long beards and flowing robes. If we ran into such figures in our travels, we would not be surprised to discover that they had very different religious and political beliefs from our own; we would, indeed, expect it, and make every effort to understand their exact meaning and to avoid giving unintended cultural offense. We might even think these men more foreign, in the sense of more remote from our concerns, than they are in reality.

But the men who actually hijacked the planes on September 11, 2001—men such as Hanji Hanjour, who flew a plane into the Pentagon, or Ziad Jarrah, who was at the controls of the plane that crashed in Pennsylvania—looked just like any number of Middle Eastern graduate students we have all met on American campuses or at London parties. And this should not surprise us, because that is what—among other things—they were. Mohamed Atta, the apparent ringleader of the hijackers in

America, had enrolled at a technical university in Germany to learn engineering. Other hijackers also fit this pattern: They were Western-educated, spoke English or German, and had modern American tastes in several respects. Their friends and families, now baffled by what has happened, often say things like: "But he loved America—everything from jeans to hamburgers." If we had met them, we would probably have thought them more American than, as it turns out, they were in reality.

Islam has learned more about the West than the West has about Islam.

Cultural appearances can be deceptive—especially when people move in two cultures simultaneously. Islam and the West have been living in close proximity for 1,400 years, and in the last 200 years there has been a good deal of cultural interpenetration. In this process, Islam has learned more about the West than the West has about Islam. Despite the scrupulous work of Islamic scholars, . . . the sheer practical impact of the expanding West on the rest of the world has meant that more ordinary Muslims have some sort of cultural sense of America than ordinary Americans do of the Islamic world. In the last thirty years especially, a combination of immigration, Hollywood, the open doors of American academia, and the rise of multinational corporations has meant that millions of Muslims have been absorbing the West's cultural messages.

Adopting Western ways

Does that mean they have become Western or American? In some cases, it does. Many Muslim Arabs have settled in the West, married Americans, gradually adopted American mores, and become Americans with only the slightest trace of hyphenation. Over time they may well develop a distinctively American version of Islam and export it back to the Muslim heartland of the Middle East—just as American Catholics, by adapting to the originally Protestant liberalism of the United States a hundred years ago, helped by their growing influence to shift the Vatican in a liberal direction.

Whether that is the dominant response, however, will depend inter alia on what America and Americans do. For, as Mohamed Atta and his colleagues demonstrate all too horribly, there are other cultural possibilities for those living in two worlds. Some fiercely reject the new society into which they have moved. Its culture may strike them as corrupt or godless; its prosperity and power may awaken resentment rather than gratitude; and its internal critics may prove hospitable and persuasive. Whatever the reason, some people reject an American future and ricochet backwards into their own tradition—except, of course, that the tradition they seek is no longer the uncomplicatedly comforting one of their youth but one subtly distorted by their rejection of American modernity.

At some point in his life—a *Wall Street Journal* article dates it in the mid 1990s—Atta became a born-again Muslim. He rediscovered his religion and his cultural roots: "He grew a traditional beard. He interrupted his graduate studies in 1995 to make a pilgrimage to the holy city of Mecca in Saudi Arabia. In 1996, at the age of 27, he made out a will requesting a strict Muslim funeral. Women, especially pregnant women, and 'unclean people' were to be excluded. Mourners were instructed not to cry."

The Islam to which Atta "returned," however, was not one of the relatively relaxed strains available in the Arab world, but radical Islamism. This is a harsh, puritanical, politicized version of Islam, which—while it claims to return to the first traditions of the religion—actually couples them to radical strains in Western political thought. As United Press International commentator James C. Bennett has observed, radical Islamism is the "bastard child" of fundamentalist Islam and of the neo-Marxist theories of dependency that explain Third World poverty as the result of Western exploitation. These neo-Marxist theories are transparent nonsense—they are refuted by a mountain of evidence, notably by the fact that the European colonial powers grew richer, not poorer, after losing their colonies—but for someone from the Middle East, they are very comforting. In one fell swoop they account for the long decline of Islamic civilization after a millennium of great achievement, for the failure of today's Muslim societies to modernize and prosper, for the corrupt and cruel dictatorships that govern them, for their inability to "solve" the "problem" of Israel, and for the political and cultural dominance of the West. They offer the ever-soothing, catch-all explanation: "We wuz robbed."

And the Islamic fundamentalism that incorporates such theories might have had a further attraction for Atta. They reflected an experience that, in some respects, was like his own. As Daniel Pipes pointed out six years ago in *First Things*, radical Islamism was the invention of Westernized intellectuals at home in both Islam and the West—and sometimes more at home in the West:

> Turabi of the Sudan has advanced degrees from the University of London and the Sorbonne . . . Abbasi Madani, a leader of Algeria's Islamic Salvation Front (FIS), received a doctorate in education from the University of London. His Tunisian counterpart, Rashid al-Ghannushi, spent a year in France and since 1993 makes his home in Great Britain . . . Mousa Mohamed Abu Marzook, the head of Hamas's political committee, has lived in the United States since 1980, [and] has a doctorate in engineering from Louisiana State University . . .

As might be expected, the Islam shaped by such people is not a gentle recovery of tradition but an Islam reshaped into an aggressive modern ideology in the light of Western experience. In all sorts of ways, argues Pipes, they import Western concepts into Islamic practice. They seek to centralize the traditionally decentralized Islamic clerisy as if it were the Catholic Church. They see Islam less as a religion for saving men's souls and more as a political doctrine for running a society. They seek—contrary to long practice—to subject non-believers to Islamic sacred law. And in all these things they seek to increase the political power of the Islamic world as a main aim of Islam the religion.

Traditional Islam vs. Islamic fundamentalism

In the *Los Angeles Times*, however, Khaled Abou El Fadl of UCLA Law School noted a key disjunction between traditionally Islamic views and the terrorist ideologies that claim to represent Islam. He pointed out that although almost all modern Muslim terrorist groups employ theological justifications for their behavior, in fact their ideologies, language, and symbolism are all drawn from the political "liberation" struggles of the last two centuries: "Expressions such as hizb (party), tahrir (liberation), taqrir al-masir (self-determination), [and] harakah (movement) . . . are imported from national liberation struggles against colonialism and did not emerge from the Islamic heritage."

It would be going much too far, of course, to disassociate Islam entirely from the attack on the World Trade Center. All the perpetrators believed themselves to be pious Muslims fighting in a holy war and headed directly to Paradise; they were given support in this belief by some Muslim clerics; a significant section of Islamic opinion has applauded what they did; some passages in the Koran lend themselves to justifying such acts (others, of course, condemn them); and whatever else Atta and his accomplices murdered and died for, it was not solely from belief in Leninism. Some of the malign energy that inspired their crime was nurtured by the widespread Islamic resentment at the power and prosperity of the (once-) Christian West.

And that requires explanation. After all, many non-Westerners have visited the great capitals of the West, and tasted their cultures, in the last two centuries. Some frankly preferred their own customs and returned home. Of the great majority who were impressed, however, very few were also hostile and vengeful. Most wanted to continue living in the culture of freedom and prosperity even if they could not stay geographically in the West. They tried, sometimes naively, to transplant that culture into their own societies in the hope of effecting a renaissance in their own civilization. They wanted to return to the West frequently and, when that was not possible, they did so in imagination by subscribing to its books and magazines.

The difference between the reactions of those visitors and the response of a Mohamed Atta may lie less in their respective personalities than in the reception they received. Visitors in the 19th century encountered a more self-confident society—one that was proud of its achievements, and was prepared to proclaim its own superiority to societies that were less free and less prosperous. There were drawbacks to such civilizational egoism, of course. But the test of practice suggests that it invited admiration, whereas the West's recent cultural relativism (at best) and cultural self-flagellation (at worst) seem to invite contempt, hostility, and attack.

Another test of practice is about to begin: war. Whether the contempt for us exhibited by Atta, bin Laden, and much of the Muslim world is justified will now be demonstrated in the clearest possible way. But so what? Their opinion of us should matter much less to us than our opinion of ourselves. For in the end, our opinion of ourselves will determine their opinion as well.

Organizations to Contact

The editors have compiled the following list of organizations concerned with the issues debated in this book. The descriptions are derived from materials provided by the organizations. All have publications or information available for interested readers. The list was compiled on the date of publication of the present volume; names, addresses, and phone numbers may change. Be aware that many organizations take several weeks or longer to respond to inquiries, so allow as much time as possible.

American-Arab Anti-Discrimination Committee (ADC)
4201 Connecticut Ave. NW, Suite 300, Washington, DC 20008
(202) 244-2990 • fax: (202) 244-3196
e-mail: ADC@adc.org • website: www.adc.org

This organization fights anti-Arab stereotyping in the media. It also fights discrimination and hate crimes against Arab Americans. It publishes a series of issue papers and a number of books, including the 1991 *Report on Anti-Arab Hate Crimes*.

American Muslim Council (AMC)
1212 New York Ave. NW, Suite 400, Washington, DC 20005
(202) 789-2262 • fax: (202) 789-2550
e-mail: amc@amconline.org • website: www.amconline.org

This nonprofit organization was established to identify and oppose discrimination against Muslims and other minorities and to raise the level of social awareness and political involvement of Muslims in the United States. It publishes the monthly newsletter *AMC Report* and numerous pamphlets and monographs.

AMIDEAST
1730 M St. NW, Suite 1100, Washington, DC 20036-4505
(202) 776-9600 • fax: (202) 776-7000
e-mail: inquiries@amideast.org • website: www.amideast.org

AMIDEAST promotes understanding and cooperation between Americans and the people of the Middle East and North Africa through education and development programs. It publishes a number of books for all age groups, including *Islam: A Primer*.

Arab World and Islamic Resources and School Services (AWAIR)
2137 Rose St., Berkeley, CA 94709
(510) 704-0517
e-mail: awair@igc.apc.org • website: www.telegraphave.com

AWAIR provides materials and services for educators teaching about the Arab World and about Islam at the precollege level. It publishes many books and videos, including *The Arab World Notebook, Middle Eastern Muslim Women Speak*, and *Islam*.

International Institute of Islamic Thought (IIIT)
PO Box 669, Herndon, VA 20172
(703) 471-1133 • fax: (703) 471-3922
e-mail: iiit@iiit.org • website: www.iiit.org

This nonprofit academic research facility promotes and coordinates research and related activities in Islamic philosophy, the humanities, and social sciences. It publishes numerous books in both Arabic and English as well as the quarterly *American Journal of Islamic Social Science* and the *Muslim World Book Review*.

Islamic Circle of North America (ICNA)
166-26 89th Ave., Jamaica, NY 11432
(718) 658-1199 • fax: (718) 658-1255
e-mail: info@icna.org • website: www.icna.org

ICNA works to propagate Islam as a way of life and to establish an Islamic system in North America. It maintains a charitable relief organization and publishes numerous pamphlets in its *Islamic Da'wah* series as well as the monthly magazine, the *Message*.

Islamic Information Center of America (IICA)
Box 40521, Des Plaines, IL 60016
e-mail: iica1@attbi.com • website: www.iica.org

IICA is a nonprofit organization that provides information about Islam to Muslims, the general public, and the media. It publishes and distributes a number of pamphlets and a monthly newsletter, the *Invitation*.

Islamic Texts Society
22A Brooklands Ave., Cambridge CB2 2DQ, UK
+44 (0) 1223 314387 • USA (503) 280-8832 • fax: +44 (0) 1223 324342
e-mail: mail@its.org.uk • website: www.its.org.uk

This organization publishes and sells English translations of works of importance to the faith and culture of Islam, with the aim of promoting a greater understanding of Islam. Among the titles it offers is *Understanding Islam and the Muslims*.

Middle East Institute
1761 N St. NW, Washington, DC 20036-2882
(202) 785-1141 • fax: (202) 331-8861
e-mail: mideasti@mideasti.org • website: www.themiddleeastinstitute.org

The institute's charter mission is to promote better understanding of Middle Eastern cultures, languages, religions, and politics. It publishes numerous books, papers, audiotapes, and videos as well as the quarterly *Middle East Journal*. It also maintains an Educational Outreach Department to give teachers and students of all grade levels advice on resources.

Middle East Outreach Council (MEOC)
University of Chicago, 5828 University Ave., Chicago, IL 60637
website: http://inic.utexas.edu/menic/meoc

This nonprofit, nonpolitical organization seeks to increase public knowledge about the lands, cultures, and peoples of the Middle East through workshops, seminars, and educational materials. It publishes the *Middle East Outreach Council Newsletter* three times a year.

Middle East Policy Council (MEPC)
1730 M St. NW, Suite 512, Washington, DC 20036
(202) 296-6767 • fax: (202) 296-5791
e-mail: info@mepc.org • website: www.mepc.org

The purpose of this nonprofit organization is to contribute to an understanding of current issues in U.S. relations with countries of the Middle East. It publishes the quarterly journal *Middle East Policy* as well as special reports and books.

Middle East Research and Information Project (MERIP)
1500 Massachusetts Ave. NW, Suite 119, Washington, DC 20005
(202) 223-3677 • fax: (202) 223-3604
website: www.merip.org

MERIP's mission is to educate the public about the contemporary Middle East, with particular emphasis on U.S. policy, human rights, and social justice issues. It publishes the bimonthly *Middle East Report.*

Middle East Studies Association
University of Arizona, 1643 E. Helen St., Tucson, AZ 85721
(520) 621-5850 • fax: (520) 626-9095
e-mail: mesana@u.arizona.edu • website: http://w3fp.arizona.edu/mesassoc/

This professional academic association of scholars on the Middle East focuses particularly on the rise of Islam. It publishes the quarterly *International Journal of Middle East Studies* and runs a project for the evaluation of textbooks for coverage of the Middle East.

Muslim Public Affairs Council (MPAC)
3010 Wilshire Blvd., Suite 217, Los Angeles, CA 90010
(213) 383-3443 • fax: (213) 383-9674
e-mail: salam@mpac.org • website: www.mpac.org

MPAC is a nonprofit, public service agency that strives to disseminate accurate information about Muslims and achieve cooperation between various communities on the basis of shared values such as peace, justice, freedom, and dignity. It publishes and distributes a number of reports on issues of concern to the Muslim community, such as U.S. foreign relations and human rights policy. It is scheduled to begin publishing a newsletter under the title *Impact.*

The New School
PO Box 10520, Oakland, CA 94610-9991
(510) 465-9709

This nonprofit educational organization is "committed to learning for people of all backgrounds and ages in their development as thoughtful, compassionate, productive members of society." It publishes the monthly newsletter *Synapse.*

United Association for Studies and Research
PO Box 1210, Annandale, VA 22003-1210
(703) 750-9011 • fax: (703) 750-9010
e-mail: uasr@aol.com • website: www.uasr4islam.com

This nonprofit organization examines the causes of conflict in the Middle East and North Africa, the political trends that shape the region's future, and the relationship of the region to more technologically advanced nations. It publishes *Islam Under Siege* and *The Middle East: Politics and Development*, two series of occasional papers on current topics.

Washington Institute for Near East Policy
1828 L St. NW, Washington, DC 20036
(202) 452-0650 • fax: (202) 223-5364
e-mail: info@washingtoninstitute.org • website: www.washingtoninstitute.org

The institute is an independent, nonprofit research organization that provides information and analysis on the Middle East and U.S. policy in the region. It publishes numerous books, periodic monographs, and reports on regional politics, security, and economics, including Hezbollah's *Vision of the West, Hamas: The Fundamentalist Challenge to the PLO, Democracy and Arab Political Culture, Iran's Challenge to the West, Radical Middle East States and U.S. Policy*, and *Democracy in the Middle East: Defining the Challenge*.

Bibliography

Books

Tamim Ansary

West of Kabul, East of New York: An Afghan-American Reflects on Islam and the West. New York: Farrar, Straus, Giroux, 2002.

Asma Barlas

Believing Women in Islam: Unreading Patriarchal Interpretations of the Qur'an. Austin: University of Texas Press, 2002.

Juan Cole

Sacred Space and Holy War: The Politics, Culture, and History of Shi-ite Islam. New York: IB Tauris, 2002.

Henry Corbin

History of Islamic Philosophy. New York: Columbia University Press, 2002.

Hastings Donnan

Interpreting Islam. United Kingdom: Sage, 2002.

John L. Esposito

Unholy War: Terror in the Name of Islam. United Kingdom: Oxford University Press, 2002.

Miriam Hoexter

The Public Sphere in Muslim Societies. Albany: State University of New York Press, 2002.

Muhammad Hashim Kamali

Freedom, Equality, and Justice in Islam. United Kingdom: Islamic Texts Society, 2002.

Gilles Kepel and Anthony Roberts

Jihad: The Trail of Political Islam. Cambridge, MA: Belknap, 2002.

Fatima Mernissi

Islam and Democracy: Fear of the Modern World. Cambridge, MA: Perseus, 2002.

Simon W. Murden

Islam, the Middle East, and the New Global Hegemony. Boulder, CO: Lynne Rienner, 2002.

John Francis Murphy

Sword of Islam: Muslim Extremism from the Arab Conquests to the Attack on America. New York: Prometheus, 2002.

Anthony Shadid

Legacy of the Prophet: Despots, Democrats, and the New Politics of Islam. Boulder, CO: Westview, 2002.

Bassam Tibi

Islam Between Culture and Politics. New York: Palgrave, 2002.

Ravi K. Zacharias

Light in the Shadow of Jihad. Sisters, OR: Multnomah, 2002.

Periodicals

Paul Berman

"Terror and Liberalism," *American Prospect*, October 22, 2001.

Barbara Ehrenreich

"A Mystery of Misogyny," *Progressive*, December 2001.

74

Khaled Abou El Fadl   "Terrorism Is at Odds with Islamic Tradition," *Los Angeles Times*, August 22, 2001.

Deborah Ellis   "Women of the Afghan War," *Off Our Backs*, March 2001.

Nada El Sawy   "Yes, I Follow Islam, but I'm Not a Terrorist," *Newsweek*, October 15, 2001.

Maureen Freely   "The Ignorance of Islamophobes," *New Statesman*, December 17, 2001.

Thomas L. Friedman   "The Core of Muslim Rage," *New York Times*, March 6, 2002.

Oliver James   "What Turns a Man into a Terrorist," *New Statesman*, December 17, 2001.

Gilles Kepel   "Islamism Reconsidered," *Harvard International Review*, Summer 2000.

Joel Kovel   "Ground Work," *Tikkun*, January/February 2002.

Charles Krauthammer   "Only in Their Dreams," *Time*, December 24, 2001.

Timothy W. Maier   "Taliban Demands Rigid Conformity," *Insight on the News*, October 22, 2001.

Salim Mansur   "Muslims Have Failed to Understand Their Own," *London Free Press*, December 2, 1998.

Daniel Pipes   "God and Mammon," *National Interest*, Winter 2001/2002.

Daniel Pipes   "It Matters What Kind of Islam Prevails," *Los Angeles Times*, July 22, 1999.

Natasha Walter   "The Mullah Who Changed My Views on Islam," *Independent*, May 7, 1999.

Ellen Willis   "Bringing the Holy War Home," *Nation*, December 17, 2001.

Index